Kurt Weill
An Illustrated Biography

Kurt Weill

An Illustrated Biography

Douglas Jarman

Indiana University Press
Bloomington

Manufactured in Great Britain

Library of Congress Cataloging in Publication Data

Jarman, Douglas.
Kurt Weill, an illustrated biography.

Discography: p.
Includes index.
1. Weill, Kurt, 1900-1950. 2. Composers-Biography.
I. Title.
ML410.W395J37 1982 782.81'092'4 [B] 82-47949
ISBN 0-253-14650-X AACR2
1 2 3 4 5 86 85 84 83 82

Contents

Introduction

The output of most composers can be seen, at least in retrospect, as falling into a number of different 'periods' corresponding to the different stages in their musical development. This division into periods is simply a convenient method of categorizing the music: an 'early' period, which demonstrates the composer's gradual mastery of his technical resources and the development of an individual style, a 'middle' period in which the style and the technical problems which it raises are explored to the full, and a 'late' period in which the composer moves beyond the confines of his earlier style into new and uncharted areas of music. The different stages are rarely marked by clearly defined breaks.

Weill stands as a curious, problematic and, in some respects, unique figure in the history of music since his output falls into three periods which seem, at first glance, to have nothing in common with one another. Weill, perhaps alone amongst composers, built for himself not one successful career but three quite separate ones, writing three quite distinct types of music. Such a course of development presents the commentator with a number of musical problems, not least in attempting to define anything that can be described as a recognizable 'Weill style', and with the necessity of also attempting to deal with various autobiographical and psychological problems.

Thanks to individual numbers such as the 'Alabama Song', 'Surabaya Johnny', 'September Song' and, above all, the 'Moritat' of *The Threepenny Opera* (a song which has become better known as 'Mack the Knife') Weill is one of the few twentieth-century composers whose music has achieved a really popular success. Weill's songs are known, and sung, by people who would not regard themselves as lovers of 'serious' music and who, perhaps, do not even know Weill's name. Yet only a small part of his output is known, even by professional musicians. Ignorance of the works of Weill's first, pre-Brecht, period is understandable since, with the exception of a few pieces such as the First Symphony and the Violin Concerto, most of the scores of this period remain unpublished and unperformed. The works of Weill's last, American, period are periodically revived in the United States but are almost totally unknown in Europe where, having gained a reputation for being inferior to the European works (a reputation gained largely, one suspects, because these American works are Broadway musicals rather than because their critics are acquainted with the music) they are dismissed out of hand. However, as I shall try to show, some knowledge of the music of these two outer periods is vital to an understanding of Weill himself and also his aims and intentions in the better-known European works.

At the moment, Weill's reputation rests almost entirely on works written during the eight years between 1927–35 – correctly so, in that the music of this period represents his most important and original achievement; incorrectly so in that, even within this short period, only a tiny handful of works are well known while many, including some of his most ambitious and substantial pieces, remain ignored.

Weill's musical language is so different from that of most 'serious' twentieth-century music and so far removed from what has become the most important line of musical development that it is easy for many musicians and music lovers – already, perhaps, ill at ease and confused by the more obviously 'popular' elements of his style – to regard him as a 'peripheral' composer of little importance. I shall later discuss the extent to which Weill's reputation has been affected by the various fluctuations of intellectual and social fashion and I shall attempt to argue the musical grounds for regarding Weill as a composer of greater stature than is usually considered.

Although no extra-musical argument can invest a work with an artistic stature that it does not already possess by virtue of its own intrinsic value there are, however, at least two historical reasons for considering Weill worthy of serious attention. Firstly, Weill was one of the first composers to abandon the emotional and dramatic ethos of Wagnerian opera and to cultivate instead, an objective, non-realistic, ritualistic music-theatre. Such a conception of opera has become a feature of many works written since 1950 and Weill has had an inestimable influence on the development of this form of music-theatre. Thanks to his association with Brecht, this kind of music-theatre and the kind of techniques employed in it have come to be called 'Brechtian', although many of the ideas and techniques employed in such a 'Brechtian' theatre were in fact formulated by Weill, and were demonstrated in his scores, some years before the two artists began to collaborate. Secondly, Weill deserves the attention of anyone interested in the general cultural and artistic history of the twentieth century as someone who stands at a particularly important point in the development of modern thought. While no artists live and create in a vacuum, removed from the social and artistic currents of their time, some seem to reflect their age more clearly than others. Living in Germany during the inter-war years, in a Berlin which was, for a short period, the centre of European thought, Weill stands at the point where many of the most important artistic, intellectual, political, social and historical currents of the century meet. Although a minor master, Weill – more than Schoenberg, Stravinsky or the other giants of twentieth-century music – is one of the key figures in the general history of our times.

I have avoided the paraphernalia of footnotes in the following chapters by listing sources by chapter at the end of the book. Although all sources are indicated in this way I must here acknowledge a particular debt to the work of David Drew who, almost alone among musicologists, has championed Weill's cause for many years and whose work provides the most perceptive and often the only source of scholarly information about Weill's output. I have drawn extensively on Mr Drew's editions of writings by and on Weill, on his own published articles and have been deeply influenced in my own view of Weill by his work. My thanks are due to Howard Davies and Pat Carter, who were kind enough to advise me on certain points, to Jonathan Reed, the results of whose picture research form the most fascinating part of what follows, to Caroline Schuck and Alexandra Artley of Orbis Publishing and to Mrs Christine Ratcliffe who typed the manuscript.

My thanks are also due to the librarians and the staff of the Royal Northern College of Music, the Henry Watson Music Library in Manchester and the Hebden Bridge Library for their help and to Mr Eric Forder of Universal Edition, London.

My especial thanks go to Mrs Susan Davies, who translated a number of German texts for me, and, as always, to my long-suffering wife to whom this book is dedicated.

Part One
The Man and His Times

Chapter 1
The Early Years

The Weill family emanated from the Baden area of south-west Germany and had its origins in that large Jewish community which settled on the banks of the Rhine during the fourteenth century. Weill's father, Albert, was the cantor at Dessau and it was here that his fourth child, Kurt, was born on 2 March 1900.

Living within a community that was, by tradition, both politically and culturally liberal in outlook, Weill's parents took a lively interest in the arts. By the late nineteenth century the Jewish communities in Europe, and particularly those in Germany, attached considerable importance to the music used in their religious services and encouraged the use of far more music than was allowed by strict synagogue tradition. As cantor, Albert Weill was a figure of some standing in the community. A composer in his own right, he provided liturgical music for the synagogue at which he was cantor and where he was responsible for the maintenance of musical standards. The artistic interests of Weill's mother Emma, on the other hand, seem to have been mainly literary; through her, the family possessed an extensive and up-to-date library.[1] Although Weill abandoned the Jewish faith early in his adult life,[2] he was brought up as an orthodox Jew; the influence of this upbringing can be seen in almost all his early music and was to reappear, reawakened by the experiences of the early 1930s, in some of his later works.

As a child Weill showed an early aptitude for music and by the age of ten had taught himself to play the piano (he made his first public appearance as a pianist at the age of fifteen) and had attempted to compose. A number of short piano pieces and a song cycle, *Schilflieder*, date from his early teens as does his first attempt at writing an opera.[3]

Recognizing his son's musical gifts, Albert Weill arranged for him to study theory and composition with Albert Bing, the musical director of the Dessau Opera House and a former pupil of Hans Pfitzner. Weill studied with Bing for three years before becoming a full-time student at the Hochschüle für Musik in Berlin in September 1918. While at the Hochschüle Weill studied composition with the director, Engelbert Humperdinck (the composer of *Hansel und Gretel*), conducting with Rudolf Krasselt and harmony and counterpoint with Friedrich Koch. Weill appears to have been an outstandingly successful student during his period at the Hochschüle and not only composed a symphonic poem (based on Rilke's *Die Weise von Liebe und Tod des Cornets Christopher Rilke*) which was thought good enough to be performed by the Hochschüle orchestra, but also succeeded in winning a bursary offered by the Felix Mendelssohn Foundation.[4] However, despite this success, Weill was disillusioned by the Hochschüle and by what he regarded as its 'unsympathetic atmosphere'[5] and left after only one year to become, firstly, *répétiteur* at the opera house at Dessau, under Knappertsbusch and his old teacher Albert Bing, and then, a few months later in December 1919, to become the staff conductor of the opera house in the small Westphalian town of Lüdenscheid. The work at Lüdenscheid provided Weill with a great deal of valuable practical theatre experience but did not hold him for long. Work as a conductor at one of the small, provincial German opera houses was unrewarding, devoted, in the main, to the preparation of rather trivial operettas. Besides which Weill had now realized that he wanted to be a composer. In the autumn of 1920, Busoni, persuaded by his former pupil Leo Kestenberg, who held the post of music director in the Prussian Ministry of Education, returned from Zurich to take charge of the Master Class in composition at the Berlin Academy of Art. Seeing the appointment announced in a newspaper, Weill returned to Berlin in September 1920 with a portfolio of compositions. The portfolio probably contained, among other earlier works, the String Quartet in B minor, which Weill had written shortly after leaving the Hochschüle, the Cello Sonata, a one-act opera *Ninon de Lenclos* based on a play by Ernst Hardt and at least part of, or sketches for, a symphony on which Weill was working and which he completed in December 1920. In any event, Busoni was sufficiently impressed by the portfolio to accept Weill as one of the six pupils in the composition Master Class and, in December 1920, Weill became a pupil at the Berlin Academy of Art. Neither he nor any of Busoni's other composition pupils had to pay tuition fees; Busoni had stipulated, as a condition of his accepting the post, that tuition should be free and the students chosen entirely on merit. Nonetheless, Weill needed money on which to live. He supported himself by playing the piano in a bierkeller at night.

Weill had also completed a third opera, on a text by Hermann Sudermann, before beginning his studies with Busoni (like its predecessors the opera is now lost) and Weill seems to have spent his three years at the Academy working, almost entirely, on non-theatrical music. During the same period, however, Busoni himself was working on *Doktor Faust*, a piece with which Weill must have become acquainted during these three years, and one which had a permanent effect on his own view of music-theatre.

Apart from his work on *Doktor Faust*, teaching seems to have been the only activity to which Busoni was willing to devote himself entirely during these final years of his life. Cosmopolitan in his outlook (Weill called him 'the spiritual European of the future'), passionately interested in people and in new ideas, Busoni seems to have needed his students both to provide human contact and the kind of intellectual stimulation which he required. One of his biographers has observed that Busoni, 'who frequently grudged every moment of his time and strength not devoted to work, and who considered giving concerts an insufferable waste of energy' was, nonetheless, prepared 'to exhaust himself teaching'.[6] In return, Busoni's students were devoted to their teacher, with his volatile Latin temperament, his sudden rages and equally sudden outbursts of volcanic laughter.

A description of Busoni's teaching methods has been left by his official biographer, Edward Dent, who records how, when Busoni was teaching the piano in Weimar in 1900, the class met twice a week:

> those who had prepared a work played it, while the others sat around and listened. After that there would be general discussion, overflowing on to the lawn outside. Busoni seldom discussed matters of pure technique; technique was taken for granted, and he preferred to talk about the music itself . . . his teaching was by no means confined to the hours in the Tempelherrenhaus; his pupils were with him for most of the day and a good part of the night as well. Busoni wanted to know them all intimately and to study the personality of each.[7]

The Berlin composition class seems to have followed a similar pattern. The class was supposed to meet twice a week ('The youngsters come on Monday and Thursdays' wrote Busoni to his wife in July 1921) but, as Weill himself remembered:

> there were no actual lessons, but he allowed us to breathe his aura, which emanated in every sphere but eventually always manifested itself in music. Those hours spent daily in his company are still too recent for me to be able to speak about them. It was a mutual exchange of ideas in the very best sense, with no attempt to force an opinion, no autocracy, and not the slightest sign of envy or malice; and any piece of work that revealed talent and ability was immediately recognised and enthusiastically received.[8]

When Weill first joined the class, in 1920, he remembered Busoni as being 'different from what he had expected: more mature, more controlled – and younger.'[9] By 1922, however, the kidney and heart disease which was to cause his death in 1924, had already begun to affect Busoni's physical appearance. A friend who visited him in December 1922 recorded that 'He was fifty-six and looked an old man; his noble face ravaged by illness, his mouth noticeably pinched, his splendid brow crowned with snow-white hair, already showing signs of his fatal disease.'[10] Although by November 1923, when Weill was about to end his studies, Busoni was 'exhausted and weary; illness and over-work had cast deep shadows over his noble, prematurely aged features'[11] he was still 'keenly interested in all that was going on' and 'to the younger generation of musicians he was always accessible.'[12]

An impression of the young Weill at this time of his life was given by Rudolf Kastner, then music critic of the *Vossischen Zeitung:*

> One afternoon Busoni introduced me to a small, quiet man of about twenty. Two bright eyes flickered behind spectacles. In conversation he revealed himself to be an unusually serious, clearsighted and characterful person. Busoni spoke of him, in his absence, with particular warmth.[13]

Indeed, Weill is reported to have been one of Busoni's favourite pupils. The first work which Weill wrote as a pupil, though not under the direct supervision of Busoni, was what is now called the First Symphony, the earlier Symphony of 1920 having disappeared without trace. By April and June 1921, when the First Symphony was composed, Weill had become a member of the Novembergrüppe and the aims of this artistic group (which will be discussed in the following chapter) are reflected in the socialist and pacifist subtitle which appeared on the original title page of the Symphony: 'Workers, Peasants and Soldiers – a People's Awakening to God', a reference to the title of a play by Johannes Becher. A piano duet arrangement of the Symphony was played at one of the private concerts which Busoni held in his house, but, with this exception, the work was never performed during Weill's lifetime. The score of the work, hidden away by friends of Weill who wished to protect him (and who also removed the title page with its incriminatingly socialist subtitle), disappeared during the Second World War and was only rediscovered in the late 1950s.[14]

In 1922 Weill composed a large number of works: the ballet *Die Zaubernacht*, written as a Russian ballet for children, the *Divertimento* for small orchestra and men's chorus, the *Sinfonia Sacra*, the String Quartet op 8 and the orchestral *Quodlibet* which Weill arranged from the music of *Die Zaubernacht*. That year he also started to work on a setting, for voice and piano, of poems from Rilke's *Book of Poverty and Death*; the setting was left incomplete and was eventually taken up again, in 1925, when it became the *Stundenbuch* for voice and orchestra. More importantly, for an aspiring young composer, the 1922-3 concert season saw what, for someone who was still a student, was an extraordinary number of performances: not only the successful première of *Die Zaubernacht* at the Theater am Kurfürstendam on 18 November 1922, but also premières of all the other works written during the year. The following year saw the completion of the *Recordare* for double chorus and the *Frauentanz* for soprano and small instrumental ensemble. The *Frauentanz* was performed with great success at the Salzburg Festival on 6 August 1924 in a concert that included the Bax Violin Sonata, Pizzetti's Cello Sonata and Ernst Krenek's Fourth String Quartet.

By now Weill was attracting a considerable amount of attention from a small, but influential, group of music lovers and, as a result – and thanks to Busoni's championship – Universal Edition, the leading publishers of new music, offered Weill a contract. Hans Heinsheimer, who worked for Universal Edition at that time, has described how 'Busoni had introduced Weill to Hertzka [the director of U E] and, to please the great Ferruccio, Hertzka had given Weill a ten years' contract.'[15] Such contracts were not, however, as good as they at first appeared since they

> put a strict obligation on the composer to submit anything he wrote during the next ten years to the publisher before showing it to anybody else . . . there were no guarantees, no advances or monthly payments and any money the composers were to get was to be earned by royalties.[16]

Weill completed his studies with Busoni in December 1923, seven months before Busoni's death in July 1924.

Despite his moderate success and the large number of performances which his music was receiving, Weill was hardly able to live on the income from performances and commissions. The first Berlin radio station had begun transmitting in October 1923 and, intrigued by the social and artistic possibilities of the new medium, Weill became at first an occasional contributor and then, from April 1925 onwards, the regular music and drama critic and Berlin correspondent for the weekly journal of German radio, *Der Deutsche Rundfunk*. Weill remained the journal's chief critic for over four years until the success of *The Threepenny Opera* finally gave him enough financial security to allow him to resign from the post.[17] At the same time Weill acquired a number of private composition students including Claudio Arrau, Nikos Skalkottas and Maurice Abravanel, who was to become one of Weill's warmest advocates and the conductor of the premières of many of his European and American works.

In 1922 Weill and his fellow students had travelled with Busoni to Dresden to hear the State Opera's production of Busoni's *Arlecchino*. Weill had been introduced to the conductor Fritz Busch who had, in turn, introduced him to the playwright Georg Kaiser. The meeting with Kaiser was one of the most important and fortunate events in Weill's early career. Kaiser was one of the most eminent men in the German theatre, a playwright whose work was performed throughout the country and who was generally considered to be among the most significant and radical dramatists of his time. It must have seemed unlikely that so famous a writer should be prepared to collaborate with a young composer who was still relatively unknown outside specialist music circles. Kaiser was not only willing to work with Weill, however, but (according to Weill himself) actually offered to write something. The first discussions between Kaiser and Weill about a possible project took place in January 1924 and were initially about collaborating on a full-length ballet. It was only after about ten weeks of work and after a considerable part of the music had been written (according to Weill some three-quarters of the ballet, including the Prelude and the whole of the first two acts) that the two collaborators realized that the project would not work: 'We got stuck,' said Weill in his own account of the event, 'We had outgrown the material. The silence of these figures was tormenting us and we had to break the bonds of this pantomime; it had to become an opera.'[18] Abandoning the original subject Kaiser turned to an earlier one-act play, *The Protagonist*, which he had, in any case, originally regarded as a work for the opera stage.

Set in Elizabethan England, the play is concerned with the leader of a troupe of travelling players (the 'Protagonist' of the title); an actor who, using his art as a means of protecting himself from reality, sees his everyday life as a series of imagined theatrical rôles. When he is confronted by unavoidable reality, in the shape of his sister and her young lover, the dividing line between the real exterior world and the private dream-world of his own imagination finally disappears. Retreating into one of his acting rôles the protagonist stabs his sister to death, declaring afterwards that he has now achieved the perfect and ultimate fusion of art and life by reaching a state in which there is 'no longer any difference between real madness and feigned madness'.

While Kaiser reworked his play, during the April and May of 1924, Weill turned his attention elsewhere and wrote a concerto for violin and wind band for the violinist Joseph Szigeti. The work received its first performance at an ISCM (International Society for Contemporary Music) concert on 1 June 1925 where it was played by Marcel Darrieux and conducted by Walter Straram. The first German performance of this concerto took place in Weill's native city of Dessau.

For the rest of 1924 and during the early months of 1925 Weill worked on the score for *The Protagonist*, frequently visiting the Kaisers at their lakeside home at Grünheide. It was on one of these visits that he met, apparently for the second time, a young dancer called Lotte Lenya.

Born Karoline Blaumauer, Lotte Lenya was the daughter of a Viennese coachman and a laundress. During the First World War she had lived with an aunt in Zurich where she had studied ballet and drama and had become a member of the *corps de ballet* at the Stadt Theater. Lenya herself described her initial meeting with Weill:

> When my teacher – who was also a director – decided to move his family to Berlin in 1924, I went along with them. One day after we arrived there he showed me a notice in the newspaper about auditions for young singers and dancers for a ballet called *Zaubernacht*. He took me along because he was hoping to get the job as director and when I was called to the stage the producer said, 'Miss Lenya, I would like to introduce you to our composer Kurt Weill' and I said, 'Where is he?'. The producer indicated that he was sitting in the orchestra pit but I couldn't see him. I only heard a soft voice say, 'Very glad to meet you, Miss Lenya' but I never actually saw him. And although I did get the job I didn't take it so I didn't see him again at that time.[19]

Their second, and more fruitful, meeting took place in the summer of 1924:

> I met the playwright Georg Kaiser and visited his home which was on a lovely lake outside Berlin. One Sunday morning he said, 'Lenya, there's a young composer coming – I'm writing a one-act libretto for him . . . would you mind picking him up at the station?' Well, the shortest way was to row a boat across the lake. I'll never forget the way he looked. He had a blue suit but no waistcoat . . . just a little taller than I, very neat and correct, with very thick glasses . . . he wore a little bow tie and one of those typical borsalino musicians hats – at that time very fashionable, most musician's wore a certain style of black brimmed hat. I said, 'Are you Mr Weill?' and he said he was and I invited him to enter the boat. So we sat down and I rowed – in typical German fashion I rowed him. And while I was rowing he looked at me and after a while he said, 'You know, Miss Lenya, we have met before'. I said, 'Oh, really? Where?' And he reminded me of that ballet audition.[20]

Having completed *The Protagonist* in April 1925, Weill returned to his abandoned Rilke settings and, in September 1925, to the composition of the Cantata *Der Neue Orpheus* based on a text of Ivan Goll. Weill's use of a text by Goll is an indication of the extent to which he was in touch, and sympathized with the more radical theatrical movements of his time. Goll, one of the leading expressionist writers, was also a member of the Dada movement; many of the technical innovations which were to characterize the theatrical experiments of the later years of the Weimar Republic (and which are discussed in the following chapter) were already anticipated in the works which Goll wrote and produced in the early 1920s. Both Brecht and Piscator admired Goll's surrealistic and fantastic dramas and were influenced by his work.

Itself a strange, surrealistic piece *Der Neue Orpheus* presents the story of an Orpheus, born into a modern industrial world, who meets his Eurydice on a railway station. Having pursued various careers (as a piano teacher, a writer of freedom songs, the conductor of Mahlerian symphony concerts, an international celebrity) and having found that neither the world nor Eurydice listens to him, he shoots himself.

Kurt Weill and Lotte Lenya lived together for two years before they married at the beginning of 1926. Lotte Lenya has given a charming description of the circumstances under which Weill proposed marriage:

> One Sunday afternoon I took him on a boat on the lake. He was very near-sighted; he wore thick, thick glasses and I did something and hit his glasses and they fell in the lake. That was the time he proposed marriage. I said later on, 'Kurt, would you have married me with the glasses on?' He replied, 'Yes, I think so, yes.'[21]

Weill has himself left a touching memory of the woman who was his wife, the foremost interpreter of his music and the guardian of his legacy:

> She is a terrible housewife but a wonderful actress. She can't read a note of music but when she sings it sounds like Caruso. (Besides, I feel sorry for those composers whose wives can read music.) She doesn't take any notice of my work (that is one of her greatest qualities) but she'd be very angry if I didn't show an interest in her work.
>
> Most of her friends are men, which she attributes to the fact that she doesn't get on well with women (but perhaps she doesn't get on with women because most of her friends are men). She married me because she wanted a taste of the horrors – a wish which, she maintains, has been granted many times over.
>
> My wife is called Lotte Lenya.[22]

Chapter 2
Weill's Berlin

The Berlin in which Weill settled in September 1920 was the scene of an artistic and intellectual upheaval almost unparalleled in the twentieth century; the centre of the intellectual life, not only of Germany but also, for a brief period of some fifteen years, of the whole of Western Europe. At the same time, the legendary 'Golden Twenties' of the Weimar Republic was a period of unceasing political turmoil and violence in which strikes, street fights, revolutions, counter-revolutions and political murder were regular occurrences.

The sudden and unexpected defeat of the German forces at the end of the First World War left many Germans bewildered. In the early months of 1918 a German victory had seemed assured; the army had won the war in the east and, by March 1918, stood within a mere forty miles of Paris. The spectacular collapse of this Western offensive, in the autumn of 1918, came as a complete surprise to the German people. The deprivations which the population had suffered during the war, the sacrifice of nearly two million lives and the wounding of another four million soldiers suddenly seemed to have been utterly pointless. The German people felt betrayed and developed both a deep desire for peace and a profound sense of resentment towards those who had led them during the war.

The general feeling of disillusionment first expressed itself in practical action in October 1918, when the sailors at Kiel and the other North Sea ports mutinied. The Kiel mutiny was the start of the German Revolution. The Allies had already made it clear that they would not negotiate with the Kaiser. On 9 November 1918, with rebellion spreading throughout the Reich, with Bavaria declared a republic, the Kiel sailors in possession of the Royal Palace and the streets of Berlin in turmoil, Kaiser Wilhelm II was forced to abdicate.

In the political vacuum created by the resignation of the Kaiser, only two outcomes seemed possible; the assumption of power by some kind of coalition of the Social Democrat and the Independent parties, or the declaration of a Soviet Republic under the Spartakist leader Karl Liebknecht.

On the afternoon of 9 November the socialist, Philipp Scheidmann, fearing the imminent seizure of power by the left-wing Spartakist group, proclaimed the formation of a Republic under the Social Democrat, Friedrich Ebert.

The new Republic began life with a considerable amount of popular support. Many people saw the formation of the Republic as representing a complete break with those who had led the country into a disastrous war; few regretted the fall of the Kaiser and his discredited imperial regime. Yet many of those elements which would lose the Republic this popular good will, were the consequences of actions taken within the first few days of its formation.

Threatened by the Communist Left, Ebert's government could maintain power only by relying on the army. On 10 November, only one day after the formation of the Republic, Ebert and General Groener agreed that the army would be 'placed at the disposal of the government' and that the government, in return, would help maintain order and discipline within the army. The protection of Ebert's socialist Republic from its left-wing opponents thus rested in the hands of the officers and generals of the old imperial regime.

Nor was the military high command the only remnant of the Kaiser's empire to maintain its power in the new Republic. The imperial judiciary was also retained. With its traditionally strong right-wing bias, the judiciary was not simply out of sympathy with the socialist Republic but was opposed to its most basic principles. As a result, Weimar justice became little more than a mockery. In the first four years of the Republic, for example, right-wing activists were responsible for some 450 political murders; of the twenty-four people convicted for these crimes, none was executed and the average prison sentence was four months. Of the thirty-eight left-wing activists accused during the same period, ten were executed and the others served prison sentences averaging fifteen years.

The hopes which many people had felt for the new Republic soon gave way to a sense of disillusionment. 'It was the same old clique,' wrote Stefan Zweig in his autobiography:

> the so-called men of experience who now surpassed the folly of war with their bungling of the peace. To the extent that it was wide-awake the world knew that it had been cheated. Cheated the mothers who had sacrificed their children, cheated the soldiers who came home as beggars, cheated those who had subscribed patriotically to war loans, cheated all who had placed faith in any promise of the state, cheated those of us who had dreamed of a new and better-ordered world and who perceived that the same old gamblers were turning the same old trick in which our existence, our happiness, our time, our fortunes were at stake.[1]

The first clash between the military and the citizens of the Republic, and the first test of the allegiances of the already demoralized and embittered army, came in December 1918, when Ebert called on his forces to free the Chancellery buildings taken over by the sailors of the Kiel mutiny. Some thirty sailors were killed and over a hundred injured in the resulting confrontation. The battle was ended, however, by the intervention of a huge crowd of people, mobilized by the Communists, who feared the start of a military putsch. The army refused to fire on the civilians and withdrew.

Faced with such a volatile political situation, and dependent upon an army which had shown itself to be unreliable, Ebert began to encourage the growth of Freikorps units – armed groups of volunteers drawn from the ranks of demobbed soldiers. Ebert and his war minister, Fritz Noske, seem to have regarded the encouragement of the Freikorps and similar military groups as a means of providing a body of men who could be relied on to protect the Republic against its left-wing enemies. In the event, the growth of the Freikorps simply ensured the continuation of the right wing of the German army and eventually provided Röhm and Hitler with a nucleus around which they could build the SA.

The clashes between the government and the Communists reached a climax in the early months of 1919. In January of that year, an attempt by Noske's Freikorps to crush a Spartakist uprising led to more than a week of savage street fighting, during the course of which over 1000 people were killed. In the aftermath the Spartakist leaders, Karl Liebknecht and Rosa Luxembourg, were arrested and murdered. Luxembourg's body was thrown into the Landwehr Canal where it was discovered four months later. In March 1919, while Ebert was convening the inaugural session of the Assembly of the Republic in Weimar, there was a further confrontation between the Freikorps and the left wing. Some 2000 people were killed and the centre of Berlin devastated.

While what was virtually a civil war was being waged in the streets of Berlin, the Allies were preparing their peace treaty, the terms of which were announced in the summer of 1919. According to the Versailles Treaty, Alsace-Lorraine was to be ceded to France, who would also occupy all German territory west of the Rhine, large sections of German land were to go to Denmark, Poland and Belgium, while the Saar and Germany's African colonies were to become the possession of the League of Nations. In addition, most of Germany's military forces were to be disbanded, reparations were to be imposed and Germany was to accept the burden of guilt for the atrocities, loss and damage which had been inflicted on the Allied powers during the course of the war.

The terms of the peace treaty were bitterly resented by many Germans and were widely regarded as humiliating. The government found itself in an impossible position. Although the war had been ended at the insistence of the German High Command, the military leaders had left the civilian government to assume responsibility for the capitulation. In the eyes of many right-wingers the government had already betrayed Germany by capitulating. The government's eventual agreement to the terms of the Versailles Treaty – an agreement in which it had very little choice – was regarded as a further betrayal and Ebert lost what little right-wing and moderate support remained. In particular, the government lost the support of many ex-soldiers and, in March 1920, a brigade of Freikorps marched on Berlin in an attempted right-wing putsch, the so-called Kapp Putsch. Ebert and his ministers fled and the putsch was prevented from succeeding only by a remarkable display of power by the people of Berlin, who immediately went on strike. The strike was total. The whole city was paralysed – without water, power, transport, schools, shops or administration. Four days later the Freikorps marched out of Berlin defeated.

In addition to the continuing political chaos (a chaos made even worse by the election of June 1919, as a result of which no single party had an overall majority in the Reichstag) the government was faced with ever-increasing social problems and particularly by the problem of spiralling inflation.

The war had been financed by printing money, rather than by increasing taxes, and inflation was already under way before the war ended. With the losing of the war, the economic dislocation caused by the need to change from a war-time to a peace-time economy, the slow recovery of German industry and, perhaps above all, with the Allies' imposition of reparation payments at a level which the Germans were quite unable to meet (the total sum was eventually fixed at 132 billion marks) coupled with the movement of capital investments out of Germany and into countries that were more politically stable, the inflationary spiral began in earnest.

Standing at its traditional 4.20 to the dollar in 1918, the value of the mark had dropped to 75 to the dollar by the summer of 1920. By the summer of 1922 it had dropped to 400 to the dollar and then, with confidence further undermined by both the assassination of the then foreign minister Walter Rathenau and the Allies' continued refusal to declare a moratorium on reparation payments, began a period of rapid decline. By 1 January 1923, the mark had fallen to 7000 to the dollar; by June 1924, following the French occupation of the Ruhr – the industrial area on which, following the loss of Silesia to Poland, depended Germany's only hope of economic recovery – the mark had fallen to 160,000 to the dollar; by 1 August to 1,000,000; by 1 November to 130,000,000; by 14 November to 13,000,000,000,000.

In his autobiography, Bruno Walter describes how, on returning to Germany from America in the spring of 1923, his attention was attracted by a strange notice in shop windows:

> A 'Multiplier' had come into existence. It was the figure by which the normal price of merchandise had to be multiplied in accordance with the progress of inflation. If the figure had been 150,000 in the morning, enabling people to buy a pair of gloves normally worth 2 marks for 300,000, it might be 160,000 in the evening of the same day. The gloves cost 20,000 marks more although the buyer's earnings had, in the meantime, not increased proportionally.[2]

In June 1923 a pound of butter cost 15,000 marks; by November of that year a pound of butter cost a skilled labourer two days' wages. Stefan Zweig remembered how:

> On street-cars one paid in millions, lorries carried the paper money from the Reichsbank to the other banks, and

> a fortnight later one found hundred-thousand-mark notes in the gutter; a beggar had thrown them away contemptuously. A pair of shoe laces cost more than a shoe had once cost, no, more than a fashionable store with two thousand pair of shoes had cost before; to repair a broken window more than the whole house had formerly cost, a book more than the printer's works with a hundred presses. For £20 one could buy rows of six-storey houses on Kurfürstendamm, and factories were to be had for the old equivalent of a wheelbarrow. Some adolescent boys, who found a case of soap forgotten in the harbour, disported themselves for months in cars and lived like kings, selling a cake every day, while their parents, formerly well-to-do, slunk about like beggars.[3]

Walter also tells how, when preparing for a concert, the rehearsal had to stop half-way through when the musicians were paid. Orchestral musicians told him that they 'would have to make some kind of purchase immediately: if they waited to do so two hours later the purchasing power of their money would, in the meantime, have shrunk.'[4] Money was invested in any kind of tangible merchandise, no matter how strange. Everybody, remembered Zweig, 'rushed to buy whatever was for sale whether it was something they needed or not. Even a goldfish or an old telescope were "goods" and what people wanted was goods instead of paper.'[5]

One musician told Bruno Walter that he had used his entire wage to buy a bag of salt.

Far from seeking ways in which to curb the inflation, the government seems to have taken a certain pride in the efficiency with which they encouraged it. In 1923 the President of the Reichsbank went before the Reichstag to boast that the bank's presses, operating day and night, were able to print 46 million marks daily.

It is impossible to overestimate the effect which inflation had on German society in the five years from 1918 to 1923 and the extent to which, as Alan Bullock has remarked, it undermined the foundations of that society 'in a way which neither the war, nor the revolution of November 1918 nor the Treaty of Versailles had ever done.'[6] Hunger and illness became a normal part of life. Food, which, according to George Grosz, consisted almost entirely of turnips, became the only popular conversational topic. In Berlin alone, almost a quarter of the children were starving and fifteen thousand children suffered from tuberculosis. As in all times of inflation and economic unrest, there were many who were prepared to exploit the situation. Berlin abounded with black-marketeers, speculators and profiteers like the notorious Hugo Stines who, having persuaded German businessmen to deposit their money in his Dutch bank then used the money to buy German businesses himself. Foreigners, who could live in luxury for next to nothing, flocked to the city.

Above all, inflation attacked the moral basis of society. Berlin was, by tradition, a liberal and cosmopolitan city. The end of austerities and the relaxation of political and moral censorship immediately after the war had already encouraged the growth of more permissive social attitudes. Now in the early 1920s, the political and economic instability encouraged an outburst of frenzied hedonism. Money and the belief in money had been destroyed. Work no longer enabled a person to support himself and his family. The entire savings of the middle classes were wiped out overnight and with them, the traditional middle-class virtues which they represented. Stefan Zweig, commenting on inflation in Austria in the preceding years remarked:

> A man who had been saving for forty years and who, furthermore, had patriotically invested his all in war bonds, became a beggar. A man who had debts became free of them. A man who respected the food rationing system starved; only one who disregarded it brazenly could eat his fill. A man schooled in bribery got ahead, if he speculated he profited. If a man sold at cost price he was robbed, if he made careful calculation he yet cheated. Standards and values disappeared during this melting and evaporation of money; there was but one merit: to be clever, shrewd, unscrupulous, and to mount the racing horse rather than be trampled by it.[7]

However, inflation, and its effects on society, were far worse in Germany than in Austria:

> All values were changed, and not only material ones; the laws of the State were flouted, no tradition, no moral code was respected. Berlin was transformed into the Babylon of the world.
>
> Bars, amusements parks, red-light houses sprang up like mushrooms. What we had seen in Austria proved to be just a mild and shy prologue to this witches' sabbath; for the Germans introduced all their vehemence and

> methodical organization into the perversion. Along the entire Kurfürstendamm powdered and rouged young men sauntered and they were not all professionals; every high-school boy wanted to earn some money, and in the dimly lit bars one might see government officials and men of the world of finance tenderly courting drunken sailors without any shame. Even the Rome of Suetonius had never known such orgies as the pervert balls of Berlin, where hundreds of men costumed as women and hundreds of women as men danced under the benevolent eyes of the police. In the collapse of all values a kind of madness gained hold particularly in the bourgeois circles which until then had been unshakable in their probity.[8]
>
> Every extravagant idea that was not subject to regulation reaped a golden harvest: theosophy, occultism, spiritualism, somnambulism, anthroposophy, palm-reading, graphology, yoga and Paracelsism. Anything that gave hope of newer and greater thrills, anything in the way of narcotics, morphine, cocaine, heroin found a tremendous market.[9]

The Berlin which Zweig describes, a city of feverish sexuality and hysterical permissiveness, the Berlin of popular imagination, of Christopher Isherwood's novels and Von Sternberg's film *The Blue Angel*, existed alongside the extreme poverty, the political murder and the street violence. Observing the clashes between the Freikorps and the left-wing demonstrators in March 1919 Count Harry Kessler remarked:

> The abominations of a merciless civil war are being perpetuated on both sides. Business as usual in the cabarets, bars, theatres and dance halls . . . Berlin has become a nightmare, a carnival of jazz bands and rattling machine guns.[10]

Inflation was eventually brought under control by Hjalmar Schlacht at the end of 1923, simply by ending the printing of money, stopping all credit and announcing the creation of a new 'Rettenmark' which would be backed by all Germany's land and resources. A few months later, as a consequence of the Dawes plan, Germany's reparation payments were reduced and the French left the Ruhr. Deprivation and hardship continued, and even increased for a time as the tightening of the money supply increased unemployment, yet eventually even these began to disappear. Foreign investments began to flow back into the country as confidence was restored; new factories were built, wages rose and unemployment fell.

As social conditions improved so, also, did the chaotic political situation. Political extremists on both the right and left wings seemed to have been controlled and the Nazi Party, in particular, seemed to have disappeared as a political force following the abortive Munich Beer hall putsch of 1923. As Stefan Zweig testified, 'The name of Adolf Hitler all but fell into oblivion. Nobody thought of him as a political factor'.[11] When, following the death of Ebert in 1925, the ageing Hindenburg was made President of the Republic, domestic and international fears about Germany's recovery waned even further, Germany's isolation was gradually ended and a period of relative peace, stability and prosperity followed. From 1923 to 1933, said Zweig, 'Peace at last seemed guaranteed in Europe . . . for a world moment – those ten years – it seemed as if normal life was again in store for our much-tried generation.'[12]

The years from the turn of the century until 1914 were crucial in the development of the arts for it was during this time that the most radical and far-reaching changes took or began to take place as the aesthetics, the theories and the practices of the past were re-examined. The Italian Futurists, dedicated to the establishment – by violence if necessary – of a new art form based on 'the dynamics of modern life', had published their first manifesto in 1909; between 1905 and 1910 Les Fauves in France and Die Brücke in Germany arrived at their own forms of expressionism and prepared the way for the beginnings of abstract art in the pre-war work of Kandinsky (1866-1944), Franz Marc (1880-1916) and a number of French and Russian artists; Picasso (1881-1973) had completed *Les Demoiselles d'Avignon* in 1907 and by 1909 the term 'cubism' had been coined to describe the new style which was emerging; Dadaism, which was to become the basis of much later experimental art, had appeared in America in the early 1910s (Marcel Duchamp's *Nude Descending a Staircase* and his first 'ready-made' appeared in 1912) and in Europe in 1915. Thus, in the visual arts, all the major twentieth-century artistic movements, with the exception of surrealism, had appeared in some form before the First World War. Similarly radical advances were made in literature, theatre and the other arts at the same time. In music, for example, Stravinsky's *The Rite of Spring*, the première of which caused an uproar, was first performed in 1913 by which time Schoenberg, Berg and Webern were already writing 'free' atonal music in which traditional tonal criteria no longer operated.

But although the foundations of modernism had been laid during the first one and a half decades of the century, it was only after 1918 that the consequences of these pre-war developments could be fully explored, consolidated and formalized. In the years before the war, Berlin had been one among many centres of artistic and intellectual experiment. During the inter-war years – the years of the Weimar Republic – Berlin stood at the very centre of European thought. For a period Berlin was, as Lotte Lenya has said, 'the most exciting city in the world . . . for all the arts in general and that includes everything: writers, painters, sculptors, architects.'[13] Among the composers living in Berlin during this period were Hindemith, Krenek, Busoni and later Schoenberg, who took over the composition class at the Academy following Busoni's death in 1925.

Wilhelm Fürtwängler was in charge of the Berlin Philharmonic Orchestra, Otto Klemperer conducted the Kroll Opera, Bruno Walter the new Municipal Opera and Erich Kleiber, who staged the premières of Berg's *Wozzeck* and Janáček's *Jenůfa* in Berlin during these years, was director of the State Opera. Walter Gropius, the director of the Bauhaus in Dessau, Mies van der Rohe and Eric Mendellsohn were all engaged on the designs for new buildings for Berlin or its neighbouring suburbs. Josef von Sternberg, Fritz Lang, F W Murnau and G W Pabst were working at the Universum Film AG studios in Berlin.

In the theatre the dominant figure was Max Reinhardt, who ran the Deutsches Theater and the Kammerspiel, but, as Bruno Walter says in his autobiography, there were many other, equally vital and exciting theatres and directors:

> The Tribüne, under Eugen Robert, was devoted to careful and vivacious performances of French, English and Hungarian comedies. At the State Theatre Leopold Jessner's dramatic experiments caused heated discussion while Karlheinz Martin conducted the destiny of the Volksbühne with a genuine understanding of the artistic popularization of plays and the theatre . . . What the Berlin theatres accomplished in those days could hardly be surpassed in talent, vitality, loftiness of intention and variety.[14]

Anything approaching a complete survey of the culture of the Weimar Republic lies outside the scope of this book. However, many of the artistic developments and attitudes of the period have a direct bearing on Weill's work and some description of these general artistic trends is as relevant to an understanding of Weill's music as is an awareness of the political background against which it was conceived.

German art, before the First World War, had been dominated by expressionism; indeed the term 'expressionist' – signifying a style in which aspects of reality are violently distorted for expressive ends – is now generally used to refer to a specifically German phenomenon. German expressionism embraced all the arts: the paintings of the Dresden-based Die Brücke and the Blaue Reiter artists of Munich, the poetry and the novels of Werfel, Trakl and Kafka, the plays of Kaiser, the architecture of Eric Mendellsohn and the free atonal music of Schoenberg and Berg, are all equally characteristic manifestations of the expressionist movement. Expressionism was still a potent force after the First World War (as is shown by Robert Wiene's film made in 1920, *The Cabinet of Dr Caligari*) yet, in the light of the political, military and social catastrophes of the war, expressionism was beginning to seem a self-indulgence. To many post-war artists, expressionist art seemed to be so centred on the artist's examination of his own subjective response that it had no relevance to the real world and nothing to say about the political and social conditions under which many people lived. Expressionism was regarded as 'a withdrawal, a flight from the hard edgeness of things';[15] it consisted, it was said, of nothing but 'symbolic vagaries and an intentionally indiscriminate jumble of colours, lines, distortions, words and concepts.'[16]

Following the Revolution of 1918, a group of over a hundred German artists formed the Novembergrüppe, a socially conscious artistic body dedicated to the spirit of the Revolution. The group sought to be a 'union of radical artists' which would re-examine the relationship between the arts and the public and would put into effect 'a far reaching programme' which was intended to bring about 'the closest mingling of art and people'.

The Novembergrüppe was too large and too diffuse a collection of individuals for it to hold together as a distinct entity for any length of time and the group gradually petered out in the 1920s. Nonetheless, the ideals and the aesthetics of the Novembergrüppe (and other similar groups, such as Walter Gropius's Arbeitsrat für Kunst)

ABOVE *Kurt Weill and Lotte Lenya, 1929* BELOW LEFT *Weill's teacher Ferruccio Busoni in his Berlin home during the final years of his life. The aesthetic stance which Busoni advocated was to have a lasting effect on Weill's own musical beliefs* BELOW RIGHT *Engelbert Humperdinck (1854-1921), composer of* Hänsel und Gretel *and director of the Hochschüle für Musik in Berlin. Weill studied composition with Humperdinck from September 1918 to the spring of 1919*

Potsdamer Str.
10 Millionen Mar
Belohnung!
Herren- und Damenstoffe im
Werte von 100000000
Frankfurter Allgemeine Versicherungs-Aktiengesellschaft
Jungfrau
Straße
LEBEN DER
TEN
2 Millionen Mk.
Belohnung.
goldener Ring

ABOVE Toads of Property, *by George Grosz, first appeared in 1921 in a volume of fifty-five political drawings,* The Face of the Ruling Class ABOVE LEFT *The revolution in Berlin, 1918. The protection troops of the newly formed Workers' and Soldiers' Council in Unten den Linden on November 9th, the day on which the Social Democrat Philipp Scheidemann declared Germany a republic* BELOW LEFT *Berlin 1922. As the value of the mark fell, so the value of goods, as opposed to paper money, rose accordingly. Here a poster offers two million marks for a single gold ring*

TOP *A scene from the original production of Brecht's* Drums in the Night *at the Munich Kammerspiele in 1922* ABOVE *The band of the Hotel Adlon in Berlin, 1930. A typically heterogeneous collection of instruments, similar to that employed in many of Weill's works* ABOVE LEFT *Erwin Piscator (left) and Brecht (right) with the actress Carola Neher and Herbert Jhering the critic between them* BELOW LEFT *Still from Robert Wiene's* The Cabinet of Dr Caligari, *Berlin 1920*

ABOVE *Weill in Dresden during the rehearsals for the première of* The Protagonist. *From left to right: Weill, Fritz Busch (who conducted the première), Alfred Rencker and the director Josef Gielen* ABOVE RIGHT *A sketch by Adolph Mahnke for the set of the original production of* The Protagonist *at the Dresden State Opera in 1926* BELOW RIGHT *Brecht's Berlin flat, about 1927. At the time Brecht was working on an (unfinished) biography of the German middle-weight champion boxer, Paul Samson-Körner. From left to right, Samson-Körner (playing the piano), Brecht, Seelenfreund (wearing boxing gloves), Hans Borchardt, Hannes Küpper and, far right, Brecht's collaborator Elisabeth Hauptmann. The painting on the wall is by Caspar Neher*

ABOVE *Baden-Baden 1927, the première of* Mahagonny Songspiel. *Bottom row (left to right): Lotte Lenya, Walter Brügmann and Hannes Küpper; centre row: Brecht and Heinrich Burkhard; top: Weill, Frau Brügmann, and the Mahagonny cast* BELOW *Scene from* Mahagonny Songspiel

underlie much of the art of the Weimar Republic. The belief was that art could help bring about the kind of new society which was regarded as desirable and in order to achieve this end, art must reject the subjectivity, élitism and the discredited aesthetic of nineteenth-century romanticism and renew its links with the people.

The Dadaists were the most violently disruptive in their rejection of previous culture. Dada had begun in Zurich during the war and had, despite its deliberately iconoclastic and provocative intentions, been a relatively light-hearted affair. Transferred to Germany, the movement acquired a more severe tone. In his autobiography Richard Hulsenbeck, one of the co-founders of Berlin Dada, describes the characteristically serious aims of the German Dadaists: 'in Zurich, where there was no rationing, art could not help being all idyllic and frivolous . . . In Berlin, fear gripped the heart and the horizons darkened; there were too many people in mourning.'[17]

In its violently aggressive attack on both social and artistic values, German Dadaism sought to reject everything that German culture represented, and, in so doing, demonstrate its revulsion with the society that had led the country into the horrors of the First World War. Dadaism thus became a form of social protest and it was, perhaps, inevitable that the Dada movement in Germany should have become as much a political as an artistic movement.

The Berlin Dadaists produced little in the way of painting or sculpture and those members of the group who are remembered today are remembered only because their work expanded beyond the limits of pure Dadaism. Nonetheless, the Dadaists had an incalculable effect on both the attitudes and the practical techniques of many artists. In its desire to abolish the mystery and élitism of art, Dada cultivated a deliberately anti-art, anti-romantic attitude, promoting the use of everyday materials, commonplace subjects and activities of a kind that had not previously been regarded as suitable material for artistic treatment. As a result, collage and photo-montage became, for the first time, recognized techniques, new technical means such as film were incorporated into theatrical productions and playwrights began to set their plays in aggressively down-to-earth locations. The boxing-ring setting, the projections and the megaphones of the original production of the Brecht-Weill *Mahagonny Songspiel* are obvious examples of this Dada influence.

By the mid-1920s, the tough, anti-romantic, anti-emotional attitude of the Dadaists had become part of a more general artistic movement towards a cooler, more committed – and often cynical or caricatured – style that had acquired the name of Neue Sachlichkeit or 'New Objectivity', a term invented in 1923 by Gustav Hartlaub, the director of the Mannheim Kunsthalle. Hartlaub defined the style in painting as being marked by a 'new realism bearing a socialistic flavour'. The most important exponents of the Neue Sachlichkeit in painting were George Grosz and Otto Dix. Grosz had been one of the most active members of the Berlin Dada group and the gradual transformation of Dada, from an artistically iconoclastic to a politically conscious movement, can be seen in his bitterly satirical drawings of a Berlin in which self-satisfied, bloated army officers and businessmen indulge themselves against a background of poverty, decay and death. Significantly, the authorities themselves prosecuted Grosz for 'defaming the reputation of the army and defaming public morals by corrupting the inborn sense of shame and the innate virtue of the German people.'

In music, the belief that art should have a social function led to the development of Gebrauchsmusik (a word which meant 'utility music' or 'music for use'), a music written to meet a specific need (such as music written for radio or films) or to provide amateur musicians with new works to perform. Hindemith is said to have coined the term, although he later disowned it. His school opera *Wir bauen eine Stadt* is one of the best known examples of this type of music. Hindemith summed up the social beliefs behind such music by saying:

> A composer should write today only if he knows for what purpose he is writing. The days of composing for the sake of composing are perhaps gone forever. On the other hand, the demand for music is so great that the composer and the consumer ought most emphatically to come at least to an understanding.[18]

While the composers of Gebrauchsmusik were attempting to break down the barriers between new music and the public, and thus reach a wider audience, other composers, such as Eisler, advocated a more directly political music, the function of which was to develop 'new methods of musical technique which will make it possible to use music in the class struggle better and more intensively.'[19] To such composers, the 'noncommitted amusement' which was thought to characterize Gebrauchsmusik was an indication that its composers represented 'the vanguard of the bourgeois in collapse'[20]:

> When I hear talk of the 'community-building spirit', through the 'joy in playing' then I become suspicious and immediately wonder what sort of community is going to be built and why these pieces of music, mostly pseudo-baroque, should arouse that joy . . . Baroque style today is escape into music history. Composers in this style believe that they have overcome the refined and certainly over-heated subjectivity of the old avant-garde and have acquired a social conscience.[21]

In the theatre, the new social and political aims of the arts were being developed by many playwrights and directors. By the beginning of the war the new forms to which expressionism had given rise in the theatre had become over-ripe; expressionistic theatre, with what Brecht called 'its escapism and screaming' had become self-centred and isolationist. As John Willett has observed, 'incoherence and exaggeration started to rank as virtues; presented in the name of Mankind, self-dramatisation and self-pity were inflated into a pretentious vogue'; what was needed was 'a gritty, tough, less blowsily egotistical style'.[22]

The foremost of those directors trying to fashion this tough style, and the most important as far as the development of Brecht's own dramatic ideas were concerned, was Erwin Piscator. In Germany the theatre had always been regarded as a means of presenting serious moral and social criticism; in the hands of Piscator theatre became an openly political and revolutionary art form. The purpose of the theatre, according to Piscator, was to explain, analyse and demonstrate topical issues – 'to portray the conditions of life truthfully would be enough to condemn the society that had created them'[23] and thus 'to kindle the flame of revolt among the workers'.[24] It was only by becoming overtly propagandistic, argued Piscator, that theatres could achieve perfection: 'Pure art is not possible in the context of the present times. But the art which consciously serves a political cause, as long as it never compromises, will ultimately reveal itself as the only one possible and thus as the pure art of our time.'[25] In order to create such a form of theatre, the function of the actor, the relationship between the play and the audience, the methods of staging and design and every aspect of the dramatic experience had to be re-examined.

When Brecht arrived in Berlin in 1924, Piscator had just taken over the large and influential Volksbühne; three years later he set up his own independent company, the Piscator-Bühne, at the Theater am Nollendorfplatz. C D Innes has remarked that 'the five years between his appointment to the Volksbühne and the closing of the Piscator-Bühne was the most fruitful period of Piscator's career'.[26] It was a period during which Piscator exploited many techniques that have had a permanent effect on the modern theatre.

One of Piscator's chief concerns was to develop a method of staging which, by breaking away from the naturalistic tradition, allowed the action to operate on different levels in such a way that the specific event could be set against a larger historical context and the play could thus comment upon and criticize itself. If art was to portray life truthfully, then the artistic process had to be de-mystified; the machinery not only of society but of art itself had to be exposed. To this end Piscator devised complex mechanical sets which freed the action from the temporal and physical restraints of the naturalistic theatre (sets which included stages at different levels and such devices as the double treadmill built for *The Good Soldier Schweyk*), exploited the artificiality of the theatrical situation (by employing puppets, by masking the actors and by having the actors step outside their rôles to explain or comment upon the action), placed actors within the audience, and employed film, projection, newspaper headlines, statistics, placards and signs.

Piscator's technical innovations were not entirely without precedent. Leopold Jessner, whose revolutionary production of Schiller's *Wilhelm Tell* at the State Theatre in 1919 produced one of Germany's first great theatre riots, was working along similar lines. In the early 1920s Ivan Goll, the author of the texts of two of Weill's works, had used films, placards, newspaper cuttings and masks in two of his productions. Even Max Reinhardt, though for reasons quite different from those of Piscator, had attempted to create a 'total theatre' which would involve and dazzle the audience. However, perhaps the most important influence on Piscator and his German contemporaries was the cinematic and theatrical experiments taking place in post-revolutionary Russia.

Eisenstein's film *Battleship Potemkin* was first shown in Berlin in 1925 and had an immediate and overwhelming effect on all who saw it. As C D Innes has pointed out, the influence of the Russian cinema, and of *Potemkin* in particular, 'can be seen not only in Piscator's use of film, his adaptations of cinematic techniques and his adoption of montage as an organizing principle, but also in the staging of specific productions.'[27] Similarly, Meyerhold, the most inventive and influential of the Russian theatre directors, had already anticipated many of Piscator's most characteristic techniques (the use of film, of machinery, of placards and of agitprop methods of production) in his work of the early 1920s, at a time when 'Piscator had not developed any but the most rudimentary of his techniques'.[28]

The importance of Meyerhold and his Russian contemporaries, as far as the development of the German theatre was concerned, lay less in their prophetic use of specific stage devices (Meyerhold's company appeared in Berlin for the first time in 1930 and Piscator almost certainly had little knowledge of his work until that time) than in their being the first people to attempt to develop a modern theatre which could deal directly with topical, social and political themes.

Meyerhold and Piscator shared a similar aim and a similar viewpoint; both developed, apparently independently, similar techniques as a means of achieving their aims. Thus, Meyerhold is reported to have believed that 'a performance is good theatre when the spectator does not forget for a moment that he is in the theatre'.[29] Piscator similarly remarked that the purpose of theatre was 'to teach how to think rather than how to feel'. Both observations are precise statements of the beliefs which underlie Bertolt Brecht's theories and techniques.

Brecht worked with Piscator on a number of productions and acknowledged Piscator's influence in a letter, saying: 'No one in the whole of my productive period was as valuable for my artistic development as yourself.'[30] Ernst Busch, one of Brecht's leading actors, later declared that 'everything that distinguishes Brecht's style he got from Piscator'.[31] But perhaps the most important of the politically orientated art forms of the period, and one which exerted an enormous influence on the other arts, was the political cabaret. The popular image of the Berlin cabaret is either that of the seedy establishment depicted in Von Sternberg's *The Blue Angel* or of the kind of pornographic cabaret which sprang up in the inter-war years to cater for the needs of wealthy businessmen, speculators and profiteers. Alongside such 'Amusierenkabaret', however, there still existed the original form of cabaret which had been introduced into Germany from France in about 1900. Literary, aggressive and socially conscious from its inception, this cabaret became, during the years of the Republic, the most politically articulate and telling of all the art forms.

Always to the left socially, cabaret tended to adopt left-wing political attitudes as well, although few cabarets – and perhaps only that of the *Kuka* or *Kunstler Cafe*, where the leading writer was the Communist poet Erich Weinert – were completely dedicated to revolutionary politics. Many of the most important cabaret writers, such as Kurt Tucholsky, Walter Mehring, Eric Müsham, Klabund and Eric Kästner, had pronounced left-wing sympathies and most were associated with the weekly paper *Die Weltbühne*, the principal and most prestigious outlet for radical political and cultural thought. The cabaret writers in Berlin, and elsewhere in Germany, also contributed to a variety of satirical papers – notably *Jugend* and the Munich-based *Simpizissimus* – but their real sphere of influence came from the cabaret stage. Mixing sentimental and satirical ballads with social criticism and broad humour, the whole held together by the topical comments of the *conférencier* (the compère of the cabaret), cabarets such as Rosa Valetti's *Grössenwahn* and Trude Hesterberg's *Wild Stage* exerted enormous influence on popular opinion. The strength of such cabarets lay in the fact that they were, above all, popular entertainments, reaching people that the other arts – even those, such as Piscator's Proletarian Theatre, that were specifically designed to 'serve as a catalyst for the cultural will of the proletariat'[32] – could not reach.

Chapter 3
1926-1929

Kurt Weill and Lotte Lenya were married on 28 January 1926, two months before *The Protagonist* received its première at the Dresden State Opera. To have an opera performed in Dresden was a singular honour for a young composer since the famous opera house there was the 'birthplace of most operas by Richard Strauss . . . to have an opening night on the same stage where *Der Rosenkavalier* had made its first bow was quite something.'[1]

Conducted by Fritz Busch, whom Weill had met at the Dresden performance of Busoni's *Arlecchino*, and directed by Josef Gielen, the première of *The Protagonist* on 27 March 1925 marked a turning point in Weill's career and immediately established him as one of the leading theatre composers of the day. Writing in *La Revue Musicale*, Maurice Abravanel described the piece as placing Weill 'in the first ranks of theatre composers' and observed:

> I have only once before – at the performance of *The Rite of Spring* – seen the German public allow itself to be overwhelmed by the immediate power of a work whose musical substance could, after all, hardly be immediately comprehended.[2]

This sudden change in Weill's critical standing did not go unnoticed by his publishers. Hans Heinsheimer, who worked for Universal Edition, remembers how, on the day following the première of *The Protagonist*, he and the great Emil Hertzka, the director of Universal Edition, met Weill for lunch in the Bellevue Hotel:

> The Bellevue offered two luncheons: a simple two marks one and a fancier one, including fish as well as meat in the

> fare, for three marks. All these days before the première we had shared lunch with Kurt, and every day Hertzka had ordered three luncheons without fish . . . This time, however, Hertzka called the waiter, asked for the menu and handed it smilingly to Kurt Weill. 'What would you like to eat, Mr Weill?', he asked. Then I knew that Kurt Weill was a composer to be reckoned with in the future.[3]

The enthusiastic reception of *The Protagonist* created an immediate interest in Weill's music and both the one-act ballet-opera *Royal Palace*, completed in January 1926, and the cantata *Der Neue Orpheus*, written the previous September, were scheduled for performance at the State Opera in the coming 1926-7 season. Weill also received his first radio commission. He was asked to produce a score, for chorus and orchestra, for a production by the Berlin Funke-Stunde of Grabbe's *Herzog von Gothland.*

At the same time Weill began work on a full-length opera entitled *Na und* . . . (So What . . .). He spent almost eighteen months working on *Na und* . . ., at the end of which he found himself with a completely unwanted work. Heinsheimer describes Weill's initial attempts to interest Universal Edition in the piece:

> He played the whole opera, softly singing with his veiled voice and went on quite undisturbed while Hertzka and I were following this unheralded entry of 'So What . . .' into the world. After Kurt had finished we felt that there was only one thing to do: to make this first performance of 'So What . . .' under all circumstances the last . . . I got up from my chair . . . went over to the piano. 'Kurt', I said, 'tonight you are going back to Berlin. Shortly after the train leaves Vienna it crosses the Danube. When you are in the middle of the bridge, open the window, take your score and just drop it in the river'. Kurt looked back. He did not say anything. He just took his music, put it in his brief case and walked out of the room.[4]

The opera was never performed and, with the exception of a few sketches, *Na und* . . ., which may well have been one of the key works in Weill's development during this crucial period of his creative career, has disappeared without trace. Weill later wrote to Universal Edition describing the piece as 'a transitional work, linking the period of Busoni-influenced classical writing to a very different kind of music I feel is slowly growing within me.'[5]

With *Na und*... completed, Weill turned again to Georg Kaiser for the libretto of a one-act comic opera, *Der Zar lässt sich photographieren (The Tsar has his Photograph Taken)*, which would be a companion piece to *The Protagonist*. *Der Zar*, a political satire, tells the story of an attempt by a band of anarchists to assassinate the Tsar while he is on a visit to Paris. The Tsar is persuaded to have his photograph taken at the studio of Angèle, a well-known lady photographer. On arriving at the studio he finds an impostor – the false Angèle, a member of the anarchist group, waiting for him. Showering her with compliments and even persuading her to let him take her photograph, the Tsar reduces the situation to such a level of absurdity that the anarchist conspirators are forced to abandon their plan and escape.

Weill began work on *Der Zar* in March 1927. At the same time (on 2 March), *Royal Palace* received its première under Kleiber at the State Opera, where it formed half of a double bill with Falla's *Master Peter's Puppet Show*. The work was coolly received and ran for only seven performances. It was produced only once more during Weill's lifetime, at Essen in 1929.

But a more momentous event took place in March 1927, for it was in that month that Weill first began his collaboration with Bertolt Brecht. The results of this collaboration have now assumed such legendary proportions that the circumstances of the original meeting have become almost buried beneath a number of imaginative additions and fictional memories. Lotte Lenya recalls that the two men, brought together by mutual friends, first met:

> in a very famous theatre restaurant in Berlin called 'Schlichter'... from that point on Kurt and Brecht visited each other quite often and started discussing what they could do together. I think Kurt suggested at that time that he would like to set the five *Mahagonny-Gesänge* and, in that way, the *Little Mahagonny* came to life.[6]

In his essay, *On the Use of Music in an Epic Theatre*, Brecht claimed that he approached Weill and asked him to set the *Mahagonny* verses which had just been published:

> This type of song was created on the occasion of the Baden-Baden Music Festival of 1927, where one-act operas were to be performed, when I asked Weill simply to write new settings for half-a-dozen already existing songs.[7]

In fact, Weill and Brecht probably met when Weill attended the rehearsals for a radio performance of Brecht's *Mann ist Mann* on 18 March 1927. Through this, and subsequent meetings, there developed the idea not, initially, of setting the five *Mahagonny Songs* from Brecht's *Hauspostille*, but of doing the full-scale *Mahagonny* opera. According to a letter from Weill to his publishers, the outline plan of the *Mahagonny* opera must have been written during March and April 1927. From March to August 1927 Weill was hard at work on the score of *Der Zar lässt sich photographieren* (a one-act opera on a libretto by Georg Kaiser) and it was while engaged on this, and simultaneously planning *Der Aufstieg und Fall der Stadt Mahagonny (The Rise and Fall of the City of Mahagonny)*, that he received a commission from the committee of the Baden-Baden Festival of German Chamber Music to write a short one-act opera. Having considered a number of possible subjects, Weill decided to set the five *Mahagonny Songs* from the *Hauspostille*, using the Baden-Baden commission as a preliminary study for the opera. The decision to set the *Mahagonny Songs* thus came from Weill, not Brecht, and was made at a time when the full-length opera *The Rise and Fall of the City of Mahagonny* was already planned. In his own 1930 *Notes on Mahagonny*, Weill says that he saw the setting of the *Mahagonny Songs* as a 'way of moving the project forward' and as a chance of exploring a musical style on which he 'had an idea but needed to try it out'.[8]

The resulting *Mahagonny Songspiel* was written in May 1927. According to Lotte Lenya, the 'Alabama Song' was originally written for her own, untrained, voice.[9]

According to David Drew, the *Songspiel*, like the later *Mahagonny* opera, was written for professional singers and it was only later that Weill decided that one of the two female rôles should be sung by his wife, Lotte Lenya (the other was sung by Irene Eden).[10]

At all events, Brecht agreed that Lenya should sing the part. His only comment after hearing her sing the 'Alabama Song' for the first time was to ask her to make her gestures 'not so Egyptian'.[11]

The *Mahagonny Songspiel* had its première at the Baden-Baden Festival on 18 July 1927 as part of a programme of short chamber operas. The rest of the programme consisted of Milhaud's *The Rape of Europe*, Ernst Toch's *The Princess and the Pea* and Hindemith's *Hin und Zurück*. Caspar Neher, an old friend of Brecht's from his childhood days in Augsburg, had designed a set which consisted of a boxing ring and a screen onto which slides were projected. The *Songspiel* created a sensation. As Lotte Lenya remembers:

> Our little *Mahagonny* was preceded and followed by the most austere forms of modern chamber music, mostly atonal.
>
> But that sophisticated international audience stared in bewilderment when the stage hands began to set up a boxing ring on the stage. The buzz increased as the singers, dressed as the worst hoodlums and 'frails' climbed through the ropes, a giant Caspar Neher projection flashed on the screen hung behind the ring and *Mahagonny* began – with a real, an unmistakable tune. The demonstration began as we were singing the last song, and waving placards – mine said 'For Weill' – with the whole audience on its feet cheering and booing and whistling. Brecht had thoughtfully provided us with whistles of our own, so we stood there defiantly whistling back. Later I walked into the lobby of the fashionable hotel where most of the audience went for drinks after the performance, and found a frenzied discussion in progress. Suddenly I felt a slap on the back, accompanied by a booming laugh: 'Is here no telephone?' (a line from one of the songs). It was Otto Klemperer. With that the whole room was singing the 'Benares Song' and I knew that the battle was won.[12]

Back in Berlin after the Baden-Baden Festival, Weill and Brecht continued their work on the *Mahagonny* opera, meeting almost daily during the late summer and autumn of 1927. While still working on the details of the *Mahagonny* libretto, Weill was also busy with other projects including the incidental music for productions of Strindberg's *Gustav II* and for Arnolt Bronnen's *Katalaunische Schlacht* (to be directed by Leopold Jessner at the State Theatre), a setting of another Brecht poem from the *Hauspostille* collection and, in April 1928, the composition of the incidental music for a production by Erwin Piscator. The Brecht setting, *Vom Tod im Wald* for bass and orchestra, had its first performance at a concert given by the Berlin Philharmonic with the solo part sung by Heinrich Hermanns, on 23 November 1927. The Piscator production (of *Konjunktur*, Leo Lania's 'comedy of economics') opened at Piscator's new Theater am Nollendorfplatz, where it played 'for four weeks to dwindling houses'.[13]

Other, more important, projects now interrupted Weill's work on the *Mahagonny* opera. It was through the impresario Ernst Robert Aufricht, who had started life in the theatre as an actor in Dresden, that Weill came to be involved in these other schemes. As the son of a wealthy father, Aufricht had attempted to further his acting career in Berlin by contributing money to 'Die Truppe', a repertory company run by Berthold Viertel, the director upon whom Christopher Isherwood based the figure of the director in *Prater Violet*. However, Aufricht remained an unsuccessful actor and, having failed in his original career, began afresh as an impresario and theatre administrator by buying and restoring the old Theater am Schiffbauerdamm. Aufricht then needed a new play with which to open his new theatre:

> We went to Toller, to Feuchtwanger and others but none had a piece ready. Finally we could only turn to the artists in the Schwannecke and the Schlichter. We went to the Schlichter in the Lutherstrasse – and there in the second room sat Brecht.[14]

Brecht was already working on an adaptation of *The Beggars' Opera*, an eighteenth-century play by John Gay, when Aufricht approached him. *The Beggars' Opera* had recently been revived, with great success, at the Lyric Theatre in London where it had run for two years. Elisabeth Hauptmann, Brecht's collaborator and amanuensis, had drawn his attention to the piece and he had sketched out six scenes of a possible German version.

In Brecht's final version, which became known as *Die Dreigroschenoper (The Threepenny Opera)*, the opera begins with the hurdy-gurdy man singing the famous 'Moritat' about Mack the Knife (Macheath). Act I introduces Mr Peachum, who makes a living out of hiring costumes (designed to elicit sympathy and, thus, money) to the various beggars and thieves who ply their trade in Soho. Meanwhile Polly, Peachum's daughter, is marrying Mack the Knife, the leader of one of Soho's gangs. The wedding is attended not only by Mack's gang but also by his friend Tiger Brown, the Commissioner of Police. The Peachums are furious about their daughter's marriage and arrange for Mack to be caught, bribing the prostitute Jenny to betray his whereabouts to the police. Mack is betrayed and taken to jail, only to escape again thanks to the help of Lucy, Tiger Brown's daughter, to whom he is also married. Peachum, beside himself with rage, threatens to flood the streets of London with his beggars, and thus disrupt the coming coronation, if the police do not catch Mack again. Arrested once more, Mack is reprieved a few seconds before his execution by the arrival of a Royal Messenger with a pardon, a knighthood and a pension from the Queen.

The day after the meeting, Fischer, Aufricht's assistant, went to Brecht's furnished room in the Spichternstrasse and collected the preliminary sketches. It was on the basis of these sketches that *The Threepenny Opera* was commissioned.

Brecht had already decided that Weill should write the music for the work and, having informed Aufricht of this decision, Brecht and Weill left for the French Riviera where they had hired a house for themselves and their wives for the summer. According to Lotte Lenya, 'The two men wrote and re-wrote furiously night and day, with hurried swims between. I recall Brecht wading out, trousers rolled up, cap on head, cigar in mouth.'[15] *The Threepenny Opera* was, nevertheless, completed by the time the two men returned to Berlin at the end of July.

Meanwhile Aufricht, who was unfamiliar with Weill's work, had been to the Charlottenburg opera where *Der Zar* and *The Protagonist* were being performed. Horrified by what he heard, Aufricht asked Theo Mackeben, who would eventually conduct the première of *The Threepenny Opera*, secretly to prepare a version of the original Pepusch score as a safeguard. Aufricht finally heard, and was converted to, Weill's music on the second day of rehearsals.

Rehearsals began on 1 August and the opening night was to be 31 August. The rehearsal period was fraught with difficulties. Carola Neher, who was playing the part of Polly, did not return from her holiday in St Moritz where she was tending her husband, the cabaret poet Klabund, who was ill with tuberculosis. Peter Lorre, who was to have played Mr Peachum, fell ill and had to be replaced. Helene Weigel, Brecht's wife, who was playing the brothel madam, developed appendicitis. Harald Paulsen, playing Macheath, thought his rôle too small (legend has it that Weill and Brecht wrote the famous 'Moritat', the ballad about Macheath which opens the piece and has since become the best-known number from it, overnight to satisfy Paulsen). The backers objected to Lotte Lenya, a relatively unknown actress, taking the rôle of Jenny. Above all, Brecht was continually changing things and arguing with the director, Erich Engel, about the way in which the songs were to be performed. It was soon generally agreed among those in the Berlin theatre world that the show would be a disaster.[16]

The omens looked even less propitious on 31 August, the opening day. Hans Heinsheimer arrived at the Theater am Schiffbauerdamm at midnight to find:

> the stage filled with shouting people wildly gesticulating, yelling at each other and only making common cause in threatening the director, who outshouted everybody else . . . smoke filled the air, crumpled papers, empty bottles and broken coffee cups littered the floor.[17]

New problems and arguments arose as the dress rehearsal proceeded. It seems that Rosa Valetti, the great cabaret artist who was playing the rôle of Mrs Peachum, had signed a contract with the Kabarett der Komiker which was due to take effect from the day after the première. Erich Ponto, who had taken over Peter Lorre's rôle of Mr Peachum, objected to the proposed shortening of his part (it had been decided that the piece was three-quarters of an hour too long and had to be cut) and packed his bags ready to return to Dresden. The actor playing the small part of Filch threatened to stop the première unless his pay was trebled. New arguments began between Aufricht and Caspar Neher about the sets, between Aufricht and Brecht about the horse on which the King's messenger was to appear, between Paulsen and everyone else about the tie which he, as Macheath, insisted on wearing.

The dress rehearsal lasted until six in the morning at which point, when everyone was exhausted and distraught, the actors and stage hands were sent home; 'many people fell asleep in their dressing room or backstage on a pile of clothes or just on the scenery or stage.'[18] Brecht, Aufricht and Weill stayed at the theatre and worked on the text; 'the brothel scene', remembers Lenya, 'was torn apart, begun over again and still didn't work'.[19] The three men were surrounded 'by theatrical people, writers, musicians, actors, critics whose opinion was unanimous: "For heaven's sake, call it off".'[20]

The cast reassembled at noon, new changes were announced and a final rehearsal began. The reworked brothel scene was not rehearsed until five o'clock on the day of the première. Lotte Lenya recalls that the cast heard that 'Aufricht was out front asking people if they knew where he could find a new play in a hurry.'[21]

Throughout most of this turmoil Weill had remained calm. When Heinsheimer had arrived at the theatre he had found Weill quietly sitting in the middle of the pandemonium, 'his mocking smile on his lips, as unconcerned as if he were just a disinterested outsider, calmly enjoying the débâcle of a crowd of strangers.'[22] 'Weill', commented Heinsheimer 'is a cold-blooded fish . . . he has no artistic temperament, no outbreaks, no breakdowns.'[23] Finally, however, the innately retiring

Weill lost his temper, 'for the first and only time in his theatrical career,'[24] when he discovered that Lotte Lenya's name had been omitted from the programme. It was only after considerable argument that he was persuaded to let her go on and the curtain finally rose to a packed house that included such distinguished figures as Otto Klemperer, Erwin Piscator, Karl Kraus, the great Viennese satirist, and Fritz Korner, the leading actor at the State Theatre.

Some idea of what the production was like on the first night can be gathered from the review which appeared in *The Times* on 25 September 1928. Noting the influence of the 'Communistic Herr Piscator' (and somewhat confused about the author whom it calls 'Kurt Brecht'), *The Times* observed that:

> The production is deliberately crude. Adopting the idea that it should be a 'Threepenny Opera', which fits in well with the tendencies now in the dramatic air, the producers have provided a dirty cream-colour curtain about 10 feet high, worked by a primitive arrangement of strings, such as might be used in amateur theatricals. Across the curtain is painted, in crooked letters *Die Dreigroschenoper*. For the stable scene, in which Macheath and Polly celebrate their wedding breakfast, there is provided only a wooden wall a few feet high and a door. The rest of the stable is indicated by means of the cinematograph. There is the occasional Expressionistic touch, such as the sudden letting down of a placard by ropes from above.

The production, remarked *The Times*, illustrates:

> the progress of a movement towards freeing music, acting and cinematograph from the ruts of Italian Opera, Wagnerian music drama, drawing-room comedy and Hollywood and creating something new.

In his essay, *On the Use of Music in an Epic Theatre*, Brecht called the production of *The Threepenny Opera*, 'the most successful demonstration of the epic theatre' and described the way in which the musical numbers had been staged:

> This was the first use of theatrical music in accordance with a new point of view. Its most striking innovation lay in the strict separation of the music from all the other elements of entertainment offered. Even superficially this was evident from the fact that the small orchestra was

> installed visibly on the stage. For the singing of the songs a special change of lighting was arranged: the orchestra was lit up; the titles of the various numbers were projected on the screens at the back, for instance, 'Song concerning the insufficiency of human endeavour' or 'A short song allows Miss Polly Peachum to confess to her horrified parents that she is wedded to the murderer Macheath'; and the actors changed their positions before the numbers began.[25]

The initial reaction to the piece is best described by Lotte Lenya herself:

> The play opened on time and from the start there was complete silence in the audience . . . it seemed cold and apathetic, as though convinced that it had come to a certain flop . . . until we came to the 'Kannonen-Song'. Then, all of a sudden, something happened to the audience, because by that time they must have caught on to the fact that something new was happening there. From that point it was wonderfully, intoxicatingly clear that the public was with us.[26]

Again, Universal Edition was quick to appreciate the effect of this success on Weill's standing and on his commercial prospects. Two days after the première of *The Threepenny Opera*, Emil Hertzka arrived in Berlin and took Weill and Lotte Lenya to lunch. During the meal

> Hertzka did something that nobody would ever have expected from him or any other music publisher in the world. He searched in his pockets and brought out at last a large sheet of cream-coloured paper. He put it on the table. It was the ten-year contract he had signed with Kurt Weill six years ago.
>
> 'This is our contract, Mr Weill', Hertzka said. 'As you know it has four more years to run.'
>
> 'I know', said Weill. The mocking smile had disappeared. He seemed tense and hostile.
>
> Hertzka took the document and tore it into shreds.
>
> 'I think it is about time that we made a new contract', he said.[27]

The immense success of *The Threepenny Opera* gave Weill both financial security and popularity. According to Heinsheimer, the piece was performed more than ten times every day during its first year, achieving some 42,000 performances during one single year.

Other commissions still prevented Weill from concentrating solely on the score of *The Rise and Fall of the City of Mahagonny*. Towards the end of 1928 he was offered another radio commission from Frankfurt Radio. Turning again to the *Hauspostille* and other texts by Brecht, Weill wrote the *Berlin Requiem* in November and December 1928. The piece underwent a number of changes, both before and after its first performance (Weill had originally intended to include the setting of *Vom Tod im Wald*) but the real problems were political rather than artistic and, when submitted to Frankfurt Radio, the committee responsible for censoring programme material had various objections. Writing about this 'secular requiem' in 1929, Weill hinted at some of the problems he had with the Frankfurt committee, observing that the work's intentions had been questioned 'by some particularly powerful censors' who showed 'a frightening lack of knowledge about the artistic needs of that group of people who form the largest part of the radio public'.[28] The *Berlin Requiem* was finally broadcast, after numerous postponements, on 22 May 1929. The performance was given by the Frankfurt Radio Orchestra conducted by Ludwig Rotterburg with Hans Grahl (tenor), Johannes Willy (baritone) and Jean Stern (bass) singing the solo parts.

In early 1929, while still working on the score of the *Mahagonny* opera, Weill also found time to arrange a suite for wind band based on material from *The Threepenny Opera* (the *Kleine Dreigroschenmusik* which had its first performance under Klemperer at the Kroll Opera on 8 February 1928), to compose the songs for a play *(Die Petroleuminseln)* by Lion Feuchtwanger and to work on *Der Flug der Lindberghs (The Lindbergh Flight)*, a short radio cantata commissioned by the Baden-Baden Festival.

The Lindbergh Flight was the first of Brecht's Lehrstücke, didactic plays intended to instruct the performers in moral and political ideas. Writing about the piece, Brecht described it as 'an object of instruction . . . it is valueless unless learned from. It has no value as art which would justify any performance not intended for learning.'[29] Like the later *Der Jasager (The Yes-Sayer)*, *The Lindbergh Flight* was designed to be performed by schoolchildren.

At its first performance, the work had a score by Weill and Hindemith, the two composers having set alternate numbers. A description of the first performance appears in Brecht's essay on the piece entitled 'An Example of Pedagogics':

> The employment of *Der Flug der Lindberghs* and the use of the radio in its changed form was shown by the demonstration at the Baden-Baden Festival of 1929. On the left of the platform the radio orchestra was placed with its apparatus and singers, on the right the listener who performed the part of the Flier, i.e. the paedagogical part, with a score in front of him. He read the sections to be spoken without identifying his own feelings with those contained in the text, pausing at the end of each line; in other words in the spirit of an *exercise*. At the back of the platform stood the theory being demonstrated in this same way.[30]

In autumn 1929, after the Festival performance, Weill rewrote the work for choir and orchestra, recomposing the numbers originally set by Hindemith. This new version was given its first performance by Klemperer at the Kroll Opera concert series. In later years Brecht took exception to Charles Lindbergh's political views and the piece was retitled *Der Ozeanflug (The Ocean Flight)*.

Weill always composed quickly and even with these interruptions the full score of *The Rise and Fall of the City of Mahagonny* was completed in April 1929, only two years after he had started working on it. *Mahagonny*, the focal point of the whole Brecht-Weill collaboration, is the most openly political and socially critical of their large-scale works. The opera begins with the arrival of Widow Begbick, Moses and Fatty, all of whom are wanted by the police. The truck on which they are travelling has broken down and, rather than attempt to continue, they decide to stay and found a city – a city which will be devoted to pleasure. The new city soon attracts inhabitants, prostitutes and men from Alaska and the West eager to enjoy the pleasures which the city has to offer. However, these pleasures soon prove inadequate and one of the inhabitants, Jim, complains that the city has too many rules. He is about to leave when it is announced that a hurricane is heading for the city.

The hurricane passes by, leaving the city untouched. In the general rejoicing that follows a new doctrine is announced – from now on everything is to be allowed. The citizens then proceed to indulge in the various pleasures offered: love, eating (a glutton dies asking for more food) and fighting (a man is killed in a boxing match). Jim, who has proposed the new *laissez-faire* doctrine, invites everyone to drink but has no money with which to pay. Deserted by everyone he is bound and led away to trial. The trial is presided over by Widow

Begbick; Moses acts as prosecutor. Jim's case is preceded by a murder trial in which the accused bribes the judge and is released. No-one will lend Jim the money with which to pay his bills, however, and he is found guilty and condemned to death. In the final scenes of the opera Jim is executed and the city is destroyed by fire.

Universal Edition had already seen a synopsis of the *Mahagonny* libretto and had expressed fears about the kind of reception the work might have. On receiving the completed opera, Universal became even more anxious and began to doubt whether the piece could be staged at all in a German opera house. Faced with Universal's objections, Weill agreed to make some optional cuts and to rewrite some of the numbers of the brothel scene in Act III, the scene which most worried his publishers. The so-called 'Crane Duet' between Jim and Jenny was one of the numbers written and inserted into the score at this stage.[31]

As Universal Edition began negotiating with various opera houses for the première of *Mahagonny*, Weill, Brecht and Aufricht turned their attention elsewhere. Hoping for another commercial success with which to follow *The Threepenny Opera*, Aufricht persuaded the two men to begin work on a farcical gangster comedy to be entitled *Happy End*. The plot concerns Lillian Holiday, a lieutenant in the Salvation Army, who falls in love with a gangster boss, Bill Cracker, and is consequently dismissed from the Army. Returning to the gangsters Lillian converts not only Bill but the whole of his gang, all of whom then join the Salvation Army.

The songs were to be only loosely connected with the play (and, indeed, some of the song texts had been written before the idea of the play was conceived).

Weill and Brecht planned to spend the summer of 1929 working on *Happy End* in the South of France, as they had spent that of 1928 working on *The Threepenny Opera*. They left Berlin for France in May but Brecht had an accident *en route* and had to turn back; Weill continued and wrote some of the music in the South of France, while Brecht and Elisabeth Hauptmann were still working on the play, and the rest in July and August while on holiday near Munich.[32]

With a relatively trouble-free rehearsal period, a strong cast – including Carola Neher as Lillian, Helene Weigel as the Lady in Grey, Peter Lorre as Dr Nakamura, Oskar Homolka as Bill and Kurt Gerron as Sam – and the same production team, designer, conductor and instrumentalists as had, just over a year before, mounted *The*

Threepenny Opera, all seemed set for a great success.

Happy End opened at the Theater am Schiffbauerdamm on 2 September 1929. At first, recalls Lotte Lenya, 'everything seemed to be going well. During the second act intermission, people were saying, "Oh, this will be a bigger hit than *The Threepenny Opera*".'[33]

During the period between the writing and the staging of the play, however, Brecht's friends had persuaded him that the work's lack of political commitment suggested that he had capitulated to the bourgeois idea of the theatre as mere 'entertainment'.

The results of this persuasion are described by Lotte Lenya:

> Brecht's wife, Helene Weigel, came out in the third act with a Communist pamphlet and read from it, making a speech to sort of whitewash what had been done in *Happy End* . . . it wasn't part of the original plan to do this and nobody – not Kurt or the producer or anyone – had any idea this was going to happen. Helene just walked out and did it.[34]

The sudden, deliberately provocative, introduction of a political speech in the middle of what had, up to that point, seemed to be a light comedy proved too much for the audience. The première ended in uproar and the police were called in.

Happy End had been announced as a German adaptation by Elisabeth Hauptmann of a magazine story by a certain 'Dorothy Lane'; only the song texts were officially credited to Brecht. No-one was deceived by the credit given to the enigmatic Miss Lane, however, ('the comedy is so slipshod that it can only be by Brecht', wrote one critic) and the drama critics – many of whom welcomed an opportunity of attacking Brecht – wrote savage reviews.[35] A potential success was turned into a resounding flop and the work was withdrawn after a few performances. Brecht never admitted authorship of the piece and even today copies of the script and the score credit the non-existent Dorothy Lane as the source.

By the summer of 1929 the negotiations for the première of *Mahagonny* were finally concluded. Weill's hope that the work would receive its first performance under Klemperer at the Kroll Opera had come to nothing and instead an agreement had been reached with the Leipzig Opera House. The première was scheduled for March 1930 and it had been agreed that Brecht and Weill would attend and supervise the rehearsals.

However, the political and economic situations were to change radically in the six months that elapsed between the première of *Happy End* and the first performance of *The Rise and Fall of the City of Mahagonny*. By the end of the year, as a result of the Wall Street Crash on 29 October 1929, not only the German economy but the economy of the whole of the Western world lay in ruins.

Chapter 4
1930-1935

Although the full extent of the economic depression which followed the Wall Street Crash only became evident towards the end of 1930, some effects began to make themselves felt almost immediately. Bankruptcies and suicides resulting from bankruptcies soon became commonplace; factories began to close and to lay off workers; the number of the unemployed, which had been negligible during the apparently prosperous years of the later 1920s, began to climb steadily again. At the time of the Wall Street Crash, Germany had had 1,320,000 unemployed. By January 1930 the figure had risen to two-and-a-half million and, by September of that year, stood at three million. Within the next two years the number of unemployed would climb still further until, at its highest point, in the early months of both 1932 and 1933, it stood at over six million. Many of the unemployed were also homeless and were driven to settle in one of the many 'tent towns' that sprang up around Berlin. Those people still in work were forced to accept drastic cuts in their wages as a means of staying employed.

The economic crisis inevitably produced a political crisis as the differences between the parties forming the coalition government widened. As the number of those unemployed grew, the payment of unemployment benefits became the particular focus of political argument: the right-wing parties, arguing that the country could not afford such benefits, demanded cuts; the left-wing demanded that the benefits be financed by increasing the taxes paid by employers. Finally, in March 1930, the coalition government collapsed.

A new cabinet under Heinrich Brüning attempted to implement a programme of austerity. On 16 July 1930, the Reichstag refused to agree to such a programme, whereupon Brüning dissolved the Reichstag by presidential decree and announced 14 September as the date of elections for a new Reichstag.

In addition, there remained the problem of the Treaty of Versailles, still the cause of much bitterness and resentment. The question of Germany's reparation payments had never been completely settled and negotiations between the Germans and the Allies had dragged on throughout the late 1920s. When the Young Plan of 1929 finally fixed the total sum of Germany's reparation payments, the right-wing mounted a violent campaign of opposition to the Plan. One of the leaders of this opposition was Alfred Hugenberg, the leader of the National Party. A man of considerable wealth and influence, with financial interests in newspapers, advertising and film companies, Hugenberg needed someone who could gain mass support for his campaign. He turned to Adolf Hitler. With the financial backing of Hugenberg and the publicity offered by Hugenberg's chain of newspapers, Hitler turned himself into a national figure. The Nazi Party (which during the previous period of prosperity had declined to a point at which it had little political significance) had thus re-established itself and had begun to re-emerge as a political force before 1930. With the sudden collapse of the economy following the Wall Street Crash and with the population becoming more and more fearful as the economic depression deepened, the Nazis found themselves faced with a situation which they were well prepared to exploit. With large numbers of the unemployed rallying to the Nazi cause, Hitler reinforced and reorganized his Stormtroopers and, in 1930, began the first of the series of long and violent campaigns which, three years later, were to bring him to power.

During the spring of 1930, Weill was engaged on the composition of *Der Jasager*, an opera for schools on a text which Brecht had adapted from a Japanese Nō play. Brecht's adaptation is largely identical with Elisabeth Hauptmann's translation of the English version of *Taniko* by Arthur Waley. The sketches of *Der Jasager* were made in January 1930 and the piece was composed between April and May. In the months between the sketching out and the composition of *Der Jasager*, Weill was busy with the preparations for the Leipzig première and the subsequent Kassel production of *Mahagonny*. Commissioned by the Berlin Neue Musik 1930 Festival, the successor to the Baden-Baden Festival, *Der Jasager* was to be one of a number of works written specifically for children; Hindemith (who contributed

Wir bauen eine Stadt – We Build A City), Dessau and Toch were to be among the other composers represented. Writing about the piece in *Die Szene* in August 1930 Weill said:

> An opera can be an education for a composer or for a generation of composers. Now, when we are trying to find a new basis for 'opera' as a form and to redraw the boundaries within which it operates, it is important that we concern ourselves first and foremost with the content and structure of new kinds of music theatre . . . An opera can also be an education in the interpretation of opera . . . in this sense a school opera can serve as a study for opera schools, helping to train singers to achieve a simplicity and naturalness . . .
>
> In a third sense a 'school opera' is an opera for use in schools – an attempt to create a piece which is not an end in itself but at the service of an institution which needs and values new music . . . For this reason I have written *Der Jasager* in such a way that all the parts (choral, orchestral and solo parts) can be taken by students and that these students can also design the stage set and the costumes. The score is also designed to accommodate the possible instruments in a school orchestra: strings (without violas) and two pianos, and then, at will, three wind instruments (flute, clarinet, saxophone), percussion and plucked instruments.
>
> I do not believe that one should think about the difficulties of the music for a school opera to such an extent that one writes a particularly 'childish', easily learned piece. The music of a school opera must be capable of being studied for a long period of time. It is in the studying of the work that its practical value lies and the performance of such a piece is far less important than the education derived from rehearsing it.[1]

In the event *Der Jasager* was performed outside the Festival. Following an attempt by the Festival committee (which included Hindemith) to censor Brecht's *Die Massnahme*, a Lehrstück which was to have been performed with music by Hans Eisler, (the Festival directorate rejecting the work on the grounds that the text was 'artistically mediocre'), Weill withdrew *Der Jasager* in protest. The piece received its first performance in the studio of Berlin Radio on 24 June 1930.

David Drew has described *Der Jasager* as being Weill's greatest success up to that date, greater than that of *The Threepenny Opera*.[2]

Adopted, and officially encouraged, by the Music Education Department of the Ministry of Culture – the head of which was Leo Kestenberg, a former piano pupil of Busoni – the work was performed by schools throughout Germany. Hans Heinsheimer, who mounted a production with schoolchildren in a poor district of Vienna, remembers the extraordinary success and effect which the work had:

> Never have I seen an audience so deeply moved as by the simple lines and primitive melodies of this score . . . I can still hear the music, the little voice trembling with excitement, the sob of the mother in the audience, the violent storm of applause.[3]

Drew has persuasively argued that this success rested on a misunderstanding of the apparently anti-humanitarian moral of the piece and has pointed out that the work's great popularity (it received over 100 productions in Germany between June 1930 and the end of 1932) itself carried ominous implications, resting, as it did, on the belief that the work sanctioned the submission of the individual will to the demands of a cause.[4] The piece caused much ideological confusion. Some critics saw it as a deeply religious piece; others, such as the critics of *Die Weltbühne*, many of whom were personal friends of Brecht's, denounced it as demonstrating 'all the evil ingredients of reactionary thinking, founded on senseless authority. This "Yes-sayer" reminds us of those during the war.'[5] Brecht responded to such criticism by writing a companion piece, *Der Neinsager (The No-Sayer)*, and said that they should be performed together.

Certainly the moral of *Der Jasager* is ambiguous and can be seen as commending the submission of the individual to the demands of an abstract cause. Neither Brecht nor Weill were likely to have felt much sympathy towards such an interpretation, however, for, by April 1930, when Weill began work on the composition of *Der Jasager*, *Mahagonny* had received its first performance and both poet and composer had had direct experience of the ugliness that can result when individual morality becomes subservient to an overwhelming belief in a cause.

The first performance of *The Rise and Fall of the City of Mahagonny* took place in Leipzig on 9 March 1930. Hans Heinsheimer was in Leipzig for the dress rehearsal on 8 March and was already conscious of 'a strange and unknown tension in the theatre'.[6]

Worried by the tense atmosphere Heinsheimer went to Brecher, the conductor, and warned him, 'I have the feeling that we are playing this opera on a powder keg.'[7] Brecher is reported to have said that, as a musician, his interest was in the score: he knew nothing about politics. On the night of the première Heinsheimer saw:

> crowds of Brown Shirts on the streets (there had already been rumours that the Nazis had bought whole blocks of seats) and the square and the opera house were full of them. They carried banners and placards protesting against the new work by Weill and Brecht. People on the streets, people in uniform, were protesting against an opera before it was even performed.[8]

The first performance began:

> it was not long before demonstrations broke out in the auditorium . . . a little uneasiness at first, a signal perhaps, then noise, shouts, at last screams and roars of protest . . . Some of the actors couldn't stand it any more. They stepped out of their parts, rushed to the rim of the stage and shouted their protests against the intruders.[9]

By the end of the work the demonstrations had developed into a full-scale riot. Lotte Lenya, who was in the audience, has described how:

> by the time the last scene was reached, fist fights had broken out in the aisles, the theatre was a screaming mass of people; soon the riot spread to the stage, panicky spectators were trying to claw their way out and only the arrival of a large police force finally cleared the theatre. The second performance took place with the house lights up and with the theatre walls lined with police.[10]

A further production of *Mahagonny* which opened in Kassel on 12 March proved to be a success, as did one that autumn for the Frankfurt Festival and a further Leipzig production for the Arbeiter-Bildungs-Institut. These last two performances, however, were 'private' ones; public performances were still greeted with the kind of reception that the work had met at its Leipzig première. *Mahagonny* had become the target of a campaign designed to drive it off the stage. The riots at the Leipzig première had been reported in all the newspapers and frightened opera house managers were soon cancelling any planned productions of the work.

It was during the rehearsals for the Leipzig première of *Mahagonny* that the differences between Weill and Brecht first became apparent. Personal and artistic differences between the two men had been present from the start of their collaboration. Lotte Lenya has suggested that, from the outset, Brecht felt some sense of jealousy and competition between himself and Weill, remembering that as early as the 1927 première of the *Mahagonny Songspiel* Brecht had remarked, 'You know, Lenya, Weill must get used to the fact that his name is not on the programme.' Lotte Lenya has also observed that, 'when you look at the book of *The Threepenny Opera* there you see, way up in the corner: collaborators: Elisabeth Hauptmann (first) and Kurt Weill.'[11] However, such jealousies, if they existed, were far less important than the artistic differences between the two men. The relationships and the differences between Brecht's and Weill's artistic ideas will be discussed in detail later but some mention of them is necessary at this point in order to understand why the two men decided to part.

In some ways the differences between Brecht and Weill were simply new manifestations of those arguments about the relative importance of words and music that have dogged opera since its beginnings. But the development of Brecht's theatrical ideas during the late 1920s and early 1930s was such that he not only regarded the music as being subservient to the text, but that he demanded that the music have a specific function. Like the other elements which went to make up Brecht's epic theatre the music had to force people to think, rather than to feel.

In his essay *On the Use of Music in an Epic Theatre* Brecht demanded a 'gestic' music which avoided 'narcotic effects', 'lyricism' and 'expression for its own sake'; the solutions of musical problems were 'to be directed to the clear and intelligible underlining of the political and philosophical meaning of the poem.'[12] Weill could not accept such a restriction and in pieces such as the beautiful 'Crane Duet' in *Mahagonny*, he wrote the kind of music which encouraged the emotional involvement of the listener. In so doing he introduced an emotional ambiguity which obscured the 'political meaning' of the text and thus went against all Brecht's intentions. It is significant that in *On the Use of Music in an Epic Theatre*, although it was published after his partnership with Weill was ended, Brecht could not resist observing (presumably with numbers such as the 'Crane Duet' in mind) that he did not regard Weill's music for *Mahagonny* as being 'purely gestic'.

The production of *Mahagonny*, in which, more than in any other of their joint collaborations, the music played a conspicuously dominant rôle, must have confirmed Brecht in his suspicions that he and Weill had different aims. Both men must have begun to feel that each was simply using the other as a means of furthering his own ends – Brecht feeling that Weill simply wanted someone who could provide words which would act as a vehicle for the music; Weill feeling that Brecht needed only a musical hack.

There were also growing political differences between the two men. During the years from 1929 to 1931 Brecht became more overtly and dogmatically Communist in his political thought. Weill, who had sympathized with the social and ethical aims but had never subscribed to the openly Marxist aims of some sections of the Novembergrüppe, was unwilling to adopt Brecht's political stance. Lotte Lenya has described how:

> Brecht at that time got more political by the minute . . . I remember when Brecht came to visit us and we gave him a guest room which was quite comfortable with the usual furnishings – curtains, a rug and so on. Well, when I came up after a few minutes to bring him some towels, I found that he had completely transformed the room: the rug was shoved under the bed, the picture on the wall had been taken down and in its place there was a Chinese scroll, and there was a sort of clothes line stretched across the room from one window to another with a red star hanging from it. Within ten minutes he had completely transformed the room with those things which he must have carried with him wherever he went . . . Kurt said, 'I'm not interested in composing Karl Marx; I like to write music.'[13]

Brecht needed a more politically committed, more emotionally neutral composer; a composer whose political convictions enabled him to accept as necessary the musical restriction of epic theatre. Brecht found such a composer in Hanns Eisler and Eisler's score for *Die Massnahme* in 1930 was the first extensive collaboration and the beginning of a long partnership between the two men.

Finally, and perhaps less important than either the artistic or political differences between Weill and Brecht, there was the fact that Brecht was at that time going through a particularly difficult period in his personal life. The Nero-Film Company which was filming *The Threepenny Opera* with G W Pabst as director, had hired both Brecht and Weill to work on the film. Brecht, in the light of his now whole-hearted commitment to Marxism, insisted on making alterations to the original text. The Nero-Film Company, wanting to make a film of a work which had already proved to be an enormous success on the stage, objected. Brecht had then started a court case against the film company in an attempt to stop the film being made. The case was heard in the courts in October 1930 and created immense interest, becoming for some months one of the great topics of conversation in Berlin society. Brecht lost the case, although Weill won a suit which prevented the Nero-Film Company from altering the musical score.

The most surprising aspect of the Weill-Brecht collaboration is not that it eventually broke up but that it lasted so long and produced so many works. The differences between the two men had been there from the start and it was only their mutual sense of interdependence and their tacit, and perhaps subconscious, recognition of the fact that their own best ends were served by ignoring these differences that enabled them to work together for over three years. Indeed, the unique character and quality of the works produced within these years may be the result of the unspoken artistic tension between the two partners. Brecht's gradual development of his theories of epic theatre and his adoption of a more overtly Marxist political view simply brought these innate tensions to the foreground. Once the differences were openly recognized, the partnership could no longer continue.

By the time *Die Massnahme* was performed, Weill had already begun work on an opera based on a text by Caspar Neher. Caspar Neher was an old school friend and a devoted and passionate admirer of Brecht – even to the extent of wearing, 'as a token of sympathy and approval . . . the steel-rimmed glasses with the leather cap' which were the mark of Brecht's own characteristic mode of dress.[14] In his rôle as designer, Neher had played a vital part in bringing about the successful productions of almost all of Brecht's works, including those which had been written in collaboration with Weill. Neher was not only the finest stage designer of his generation, however, but also a man whose contribution to the development of the theatre during the years of the Weimar Republic extended to many other areas, including direction (he was to be co-director, with Brecht, of the first Berlin production of *Mahagonny*) and the actual writing of plays. John Willett has described how Neher not only designed the sets and the costumes of many of Brecht's plays but 'in dozens of sketches would suggest the action too'.[15] Brecht himself gave an indication of the extent to which Neher contributed to and involved himself in the actual creation of a work when he wrote, in his diary for 2 March 1921: 'In the morning Cas and I worked on the Webb's film *The Rotating Wine Jar*. Cas acted as midwife and took over the groaning too. He get the pains; I get the child.'[16] Little wonder, then, that Brecht regarded Neher as the most important and creatively stimulating of his theatrical partners.

Die Bürgschaft (The Pledge), the three act opera for which Neher provided the libretto, is the story of the relationship between two men, Johann Mattes, a farmer, and his friend the corn dealer David Orth.

In the Prologue to the opera Mattes, who has lost everything gambling, persuades Orth to lend him the necessary money.

In Act I, which takes place six years later, Mattes again goes to his friend for help and persuades Orth to sell him his last two bags of grain. Only afterwards does Orth discover that one of the sacks contained a considerable amount of money which had been hidden there, for safety, by his son. Orth is not worried, since he knows that Mattes will return with the money. Mattes, however, does not return and only much later, when threatened by blackmailers, does he confess and offer Orth his money. Orth refuses, saying that the offer has come too late, and suggests that they allow the courts to decide who is the legal owner of the money.

At the start of Act II the judge decides that the money should be shared between Mattes's daughter and Orth's son. During the course of the act, however, it is announced that the country has been invaded and conquered by a neighbouring power; the land will henceforth be ruled by the laws of money and of force. The humanitarian judge is removed from office and the case of Mattes and Orth re-tried.Both are found guilty and the money is confiscated by the State.

Six years later, when Act III begins, both men have become corrupted by power and by the money which they have made by exploiting the war which rages across the land. Mattes has used the administrative disorganization of the wartime conditions to steal from the people; Orth has deliberately withheld grain from the starving people in order to force up prices. In the final scene of the work Mattes, mobbed by an angry crowd, again turns to Orth for protection. Orth, acting now according to the 'law of money and of force' hands his friend over to the crowd to be killed.

Die Bürgschaft was begun in August 1930 and completed some fourteen months later in October 1931. During these fourteen months, however, the political situation in Germany had become even more dangerous. In the elections of September 1930 the Nazis, who had held a mere twelve seats in the previous Reichstag, won 170 seats. The Nazi vote had risen from 810,000 to six-and-a-half million and they now became the second largest party in the Reichstag. The new parliament opened on 13 October 1930 with Nazi demonstrations inside, and with riots and parades outside the Reichstag buildings. Throughout the following fifteen months the Nazis kept up an unceasing campaign of propaganda and violent activity in the streets. In 1931 the editor of *Die Weltbühne*, the main voice of the left wing, was arrested. SA violence at showings of the American film *All Quiet on the Western Front* forced the government to ban the film on the grounds that it 'endangered Germany's national prestige'. There was, said the British Ambassador to Berlin in July 1931, 'an unnatural silence hanging over the city . . . an atmosphere of extreme tension similar to that which I observed in Berlin in the critical days immediately before the war.'[17]

At the same time the economic situation deteriorated even further as the full effects of the Wall Street Crash made themselves felt. By March 1931 the unemployment figures stood at nearly five million. In July, the banking crisis which had been threatening for two years finally occurred. Towards the end of June one of Germany's largest textile concerns had been forced to declare itself bankrupt. The Darmstadt Bank, which had invested in the concern, lost nearly forty million marks in the collapse and, as unrest spread, the public began to withdraw its money from the bank. With the subsequent collapse of the great Kreditanstalt of Vienna, Austria's largest banking group, the run spread to other banks and the collapse of the whole banking system seemed imminent. The Stock Exchange was closed for more than a month, industrial production and shares fell dramatically, banks closed. The complete collapse of the financial system was narrowly avoided but the crisis seriously undermined the standing of the government, forcing it to demand even greater sacrifices from, and placing further austerities on, the public.

It was against this background that *The Rise and Fall of the City of Mahagonny* finally received its first performance in Berlin. That the performance took place at all was due to the courage of E J Aufricht, the man who had commissioned *The Threepenny Opera* and *Happy End*. Aufricht decided to mount the work, not in the Theater am Schiffbauerdamm, where the earlier pieces had received their premières, but in the larger Theater am Kürfurstendamm, Max Reinhardt's theatre which was hired for the run. Hoping for a financial success on the scale of *The Threepenny Opera*, Aufricht persuaded Weill to agree that the cast should consist of cabaret performers, rather than opera singers, and that the work should be cut to make it more accessible to a popular audience. Weill undertook a further revision of the score, adding new pieces and rewriting or omitting some (such as the 'Crane Duet') that would have been impossible or unsuitable for the voices at his disposal. The work had its Berlin première on 21 December 1931 and was conducted by Alexander von Zemlinsky. The production and set designs were by Caspar Neher. The cast included Harald Paulsen (the original Macheath) as Jimmy Mahoney, Trude Hesterberg (the owner of the famous *Wild Stage* cabaret) as Widow Begbick and Lotte Lenya as Jenny. Surprisingly, perhaps, the piece ran without any of the interruptions which had marred the Leipzig staging of the work as well as subsequent performances. With the Nazi seizure of power less than eighteen months ahead, Berlin maintained its tradition of tolerance and cosmopolitanism. Berlin was the only place left in Germany where the work could still be staged.

The Berlin première of the *Mahagonny* opera was among Weill's last German successes. On 10 March 1932 the State Opera gave the first performance of *Die Bürgschaft* conducted by Fritz Stiedry and produced by Carl Ebert. A few critics reviewed the piece favourably but, on the whole, the work was given only a luke-warm reception. The Nazi press had launched a violent campaign against the work some time before the première. The day before the opening the Nazi *Völkischer Beobachter* had published a notice which declared:

> The State Opera intends to slap the German nation in the face in the first half of March by giving the première of a new opera, *Die Bürgschaft*, by Kurt Weill, the composer who has been shameless enough to offer the German people *The Threepenny Opera*, *The Rise and Fall of the City of Mahagonny* and the other inferior works that he has written. This Jew has yet to realize that the last named piece led to a riot in Leipzig and that his abominable and worthless

Brecht and Weill were rarely photographed together; these photographs are from a series probably taken when they were preparing The Threepenny Opera

ABOVE *Weill's original manuscript of the lovesong from Act 1 of* The Threepenny Opera. *Weill seems to have changed his mind about the disposition of instrumental parts in this number at the last moment* ABOVE RIGHT *Casper Neher's design of the final scene for the original production of* The Threepenny Opera *at the Theater am Schiffbauerdamm, Berlin 1928* BOTTOM RIGHT *The photo-montage by Günter Hirschel-Protsch which formed the backdrop of the only staged version of* Der Ozeanflug *(originally* Der Flug der Lindberghs*); Breslau 1930*

LEFT *Lotte Lenya as Jenny and Harald Paulsen as Paul Ackermann in the first Berlin production (1931) of* The Rise and Fall of the City of Mahagonny, *which was conducted by Alexander von Zemlinsky (above left) and with sets designed by Casper Neher (above right), who collaborated on most of the Brecht/Weill works* BELOW *Carola Neher as Lillian, Oskar Homolka as Bill and Peter Lorre as Dr Nakamura in the original production of* Happy End *at the Theater am Schiffbauerdamm, Berlin September 1929. Although Brecht was undoubtedly the author of this play, it was attributed to 'Dorothy Lane'*

ABOVE *Rudolf Forster as Macheath and Lotte Lenya as Jenny in the brothel scene from G W Pabst's film of* The Threepenny Opera ABOVE RIGHT *A propaganda photograph showing Nazis being cheered by on-lookers as they drive through the streets of Berlin in 1929* BELOW RIGHT *G W Pabst directing Carola Neher (Polly) and Rudolf Forster (Macheath) in the wedding sequence during the shooting of the film version of* The Threepenny Opera BELOW FAR RIGHT *The cover of the programme for the opening night of* Die Bürgschaft

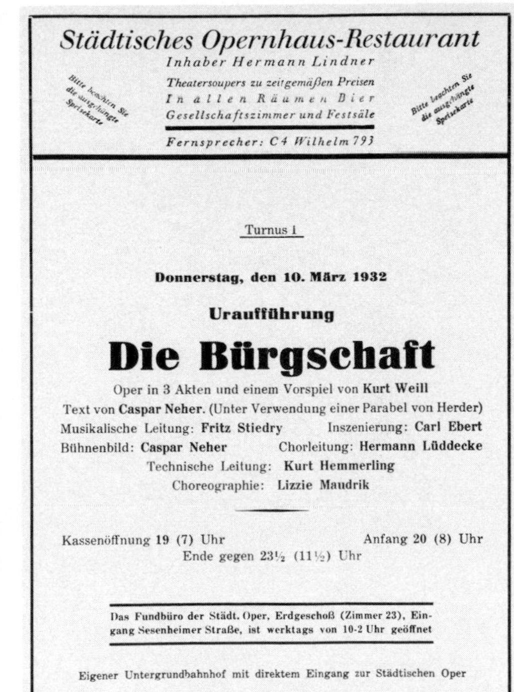

Städtisches Opernhaus-Restaurant

Inhaber Hermann Lindner

Theatersoupers zu zeitgemäßen Preisen
In allen Räumen Bier
Gesellschaftszimmer und Festsäle

Fernsprecher: C4 Wilhelm 793

Bitte beachten Sie die ausgehängte Speisekarte

Bitte beachten Sie die ausgehängte Speisekarte

Turnus I

Donnerstag, den 10. März 1932

Uraufführung

Die Bürgschaft

Oper in 3 Akten und einem Vorspiel von **Kurt Weill**
Text von **Caspar Neher.** (Unter Verwendung einer Parabel von Herder)
Musikalische Leitung: **Fritz Stiedry** Inszenierung: **Carl Ebert**
Bühnenbild: **Caspar Neher** Chorleitung: **Hermann Lüddecke**
Technische Leitung: **Kurt Hemmerling**
Choreographie: **Lizzie Maudrik**

Kassenöffnung 19 (7) Uhr Anfang 20 (8) Uhr
Ende gegen 23½ (11½) Uhr

Das Fundbüro der Städt. Oper, Erdgeschoß (Zimmer 23), Eingang Sesenheimer Straße, ist werktags von 10-2 Uhr geöffnet

Eigener Untergrundbahnhof mit direktem Eingang zur Städtischen Oper

ABOVE LEFT *Collecting copies of the works of blacklisted authors for public burning which took place in Berlin in 1933* ABOVE RIGHT *This plaque, calling on all Germans to boycott Jewish businesses was just one example of the antisemitic campaign the Nazis were waging in Berlin by 1932* BELOW *Caspar Neher's sketch of a scene from the original production of* Der Silbersee, *Leipzig February 1933, the last work which Weill wrote in Germany*

> *Threepenny Opera* is rejected everywhere. It is inconceivable that a composer who purveys such totally un-German pieces should again be given the chance to appear at a theatre which is supported by the German tax-payer's money. Let Israel find edification in Weill's new opera.[18]

Those opera houses that had been about to produce the piece quickly changed their plans and the future performances, which the State Opera had already announced for the coming season, never took place. It was no longer safe to bill such a work and it would not be long before any association with Weill's music was a danger. When Ebert was eventually dismissed from his position at the State Opera, his advocacy of *Die Bürgschaft* was cited as one of the reasons. Kestenberg, who, as head of the Music Education Department, had promoted *Der Jasager* was also dismissed. Brecher, who had conducted the Leipzig première of *Mahagonny* and who, in 1930, had denied having any interest in politics, shot his wife and then committed suicide in 1935.

By early 1932 Hindenburg's seven year term of office had expired and a new presidential election became necessary. The presidential campaign of March 1932 was the first of five election campaigns in Germany during that year. The results of the March campaign were inconclusive; although the Nazi vote had risen to 11.4 million, Hindenburg polled seven million votes more than the Nazis. However, Hindenburg had failed by 0.4 per cent to achieve the absolute majority required and another election was needed. In the second election, on 10 April, Hindenburg attained the required majority but the Nazis increased their vote by two million.

A fortnight later the Prussian state elections showed a similar dramatic increase in the Nazi votes when, from having had nine seats, they became the largest party with 162. From that point onwards, the political situation began to gather the momentum that, within six months, would bring Hitler the Chancellorship and the Nazis to power. As Stefan Zweig observed:

> Inflation, unemployment, the political crisis and, not least, the folly of lands abroad, had made the German people restless; a tremendous desire for order animated all circles of the German people, to whom order had always been more important than freedom and justice. And anyone who promised order – even Goethe said that disorder was more distasteful to him than even an injustice – could count on hundreds of thousands of supporters from the start.[19]

Because of various manoeuvres by a number of powerful enemies, and, in particular by General Schleicher, the position of Chancellor Brüning had been so undermined that President Hindenburg no longer regarded him with any confidence and demanded his resignation. The new Chancellor, Franz von Papen, Schleicher's candidate, immediately dismissed the Reichstag and called for a new election on 31 July. He also lifted the ban that had been imposed on the SA. Alan Bullock has described how, 'in the weeks that followed, murder and violence became everyday occurrences in the streets of the big German cities. According to Grzesinski, the Police President of Berlin, there were 461 political riots in Prussia alone betwen June 1st and July 20th 1932.'[20] The fiercest fighting was between the Nazis and the Communists and, as Bullock remarks, the 'impression that events favoured the triumph of one or other form of extremism was strengthened, and helped both parties to win votes at the coming election.'[21]

In July 1932, amidst this political turmoil, Weill began working on what was to be the last work which he would complete in Germany, the incidental music to Georg Kaiser's *Der Silbersee.* Inevitably, perhaps, the piece was concerned with the social problems of economic decline and unemployment.

On 28 January 1933, General Schleicher resigned the Chancellorship and two days later, on 30 January, Adolf Hitler became Chancellor of the German Reich.

Der Silbersee received simultaneous first performances in Leipzig, Erfurt and Magdenburg on 18 February 1933. The *Berlin Tageblatt,* which carried reviews of both the Leipzig and Magdenburg performances, described the success of the work as being 'very great' and said that 'Weill, Sierck [the designer of the Leipzig production], Brecher [the conductor] and the principals had to take many curtain calls' and bemoaned the fact that Berlin was not to see a performance of the piece.[22] The *Leipziger Neuste Nachrichten* of 19 February carried a similarly favourable review. F A Hauptmann, the music critic of the Nazi *Völkischer Beobachter,* however, commented:

> One must distrust an artist who concerns himself with such subjects, who writes 'music' for works which are intended to destroy art and the meaning of true art, especially if this artist is a Jew who is allowed to use the German stage to achieve his goal. The music of *Silbersee* shows that these misgivings are correct.[23]

The second performance of *Der Silbersee* in Magdenburg on 21 February was interrupted by riots organized by the Nazi Kampfbund für Deutsche Kultur.

On 27 February 1933, less than a week after this second Magdenburg performance of *Silbersee*, the Reichstag fire occurred, the event which signalled the beginning of Hitler's purge on his political opponents. On the following day Hitler announced the suspension of the Weimar constitution and declared that there would be imposed 'for the protection of the people and the state, lawful restriction on personal liberty, on the rights of free expression of opinion including the freedom of the press, on the rights of assembly and associations'. In addition, 'violations of the privacy of postal, telegraphic and telephonic communications, warrants for house searches and orders for confiscation as well as restriction of property' were declared 'permissible beyond the legal limits otherwise prescribed'.

Many left-wing sympathizers, writers and artists – including Brecht – left Germany on 28 February, the day after the Reichstag fire. Weill remained in Berlin for another month, until 21 March, the so-called 'Day of Potsdam' when Hitler and Hindenburg publicly sealed their alliance at a ceremony marking the opening of the new Reichstag. The new Reichstag elections had taken place on 4 March when the Nazis had won a bare majority. Learning that he was on the Nazi blacklist, and knowing that many of his acquaintances had been arrested, Weill and his wife Lotte Lenya left Germany by car for France on 21 March 1933. On 10 May 1933, less than two months after Weill had left Germany, the works of Brecht and many other writers were publicly burned. Weill's publisher, Universal Edition, was based in Austria rather than Germany, and his scores therefore remained safe until 1938 when, immediately after the Anschluss, the offices of Universal were raided by the Gestapo and many of the scores held there were destroyed.

The Weills arrived in Paris on 23 March 1933. Weill was already well known in France. A concert performance of *Der Jasager* and the *Mahagonny Songspiel* under Walter Straram in the Salle Gaveau in Paris on 11 December 1932 had been met with rapturous acclaim, affording Weill what David Drew has described as 'the last, and by far the greatest, triumph of his European career'. The French composer Darius Milhaud, a close friend of Weill's in both Europe and America, has described the effect of this Parisian concert in his autobiography as follows:

> Thanks to the generosity of the Vicomtesse de Noailles, we were able to present Kurt Weill's *Mahagonny* and *Der Jasager*, for which the soloist Lotte Lenya and the conductor Maurice Abravanel came from Germany as well as a group of children, for *Der Jasager* was written specifically for schools. I was lecturing in Holland at the time the concert was given and, in the train that was bringing us back to Paris, I told Madeline that we should no doubt find that the city had been taken by storm. Little did I know how true this was, for the delirious enthusiasm aroused by these two works lasted for several days. The Montparnasse set used the concert as a pretext for political diatribes; it saw in it an expression of the moral bankruptcy and pessimism of our time. Smart society was as carried away as if it had been the first performance of a Bach Passion.[24]

Reviewing the concert in *Candide* on 15 December 1932, Émile Vuillermoz said: 'It is many years since Paris has become aware of such strong and lofty emotions. Such performances must be offered to the public again'.[25] Marcel More, in *La Politique*, became lyrical in his praise of a score which had 'the consummate skill and lively emotion of an 18th-century master . . . its extraordinary qualities brought forth all the applause. A unique voice speaks to us in these works – despairingly beautiful and tragic, like the long stem of a black rose with spikes and sharp thorns.'[26]

As a result of this success the Princesse Edmonde de Polignac, the great French patroness of new music, had commissioned Weill to write the work that was eventually to become the Second Symphony. Weill had started work on the piece in Berlin in January 1933, after the completion of *Der Silbersee*. Having taken sketches for the Symphony with him when he left Germany, he now continued work on the composition. Within a few weeks of arriving in France, however, his work on the Symphony was interrupted by a more urgent composition for a ballet for 'Les Ballets 1933', a newly formed company directed by the young George Balanchine and Boris Kochno, Diaghilev's secretary. Brecht (who had left Berlin before Weill but had travelled to France via Czechoslovakia, Austria and Switzerland) had just arrived in Paris and Weill turned once more to him for a subject. The resulting 'ballet with songs' – *The Seven Deadly Sins of the Bourgeoisie* – was written during April and May and received its first performance at the Théâtre des Champs Élysées on 7 June 1933.

The ballet tells the story of Anna, a young girl sent out into the world to earn money to build her family a house in Mississippi. Anna is represented by two people – Anna I (the singer) representing the practical realist; Anna II (the dancer) representing the idealistic aspects of the character. During the course of the work the realistic Anna I is gradually shown to have overcome the moral scruples of Anna II. Each scene is set in a different city and in each Anna II is persuaded to avoid one of those virtues which the bourgeoisie regards as deadly sins – for example the sin of sloth (in performing an injustice which would enable one to rise up the social ladder), the sin of lust (which makes a woman go with a man she likes rather than with a man who can pay well), the sin of anger (which encourages one to fight a mean action, even if the fight is against one's own best interests) and so on. Having successfully avoided these 'sins', Anna returns home with enough money to build the family house.

The work had a mixed reception, leaving many critics puzzled by its unusual form. Walter Mehring, the great satirist, found it 'a marvellous evening . . . an élite of celebrated artists and interpreters such as one was used to in the days of the great German theatre.'[27] Count Harry Kessler, on the other hand, thought 'the music pretty and original . . . everything much the same as in *The Threepenny Opera*' but noted that 'it had had a bad reception in the press and with the public – in spite of the popularity which Weill enjoys here.'[28] The conductor was Maurice Abravanel; the main dancer was Tilly Loch and the singer Lotte Lenya. The sets were by Caspar Neher, the librettist of *Die Bürgschaft* and the designer for all Brecht's and Weill's previous works. It was the last time that Brecht, Neher and Weill would collaborate.

Weill returned to his work on the Symphony in the late summer of 1933 and completed the piece in the following February, by which time the Weills had acquired a house in the village of Louveciennes. Arno Huth has left a description of the house in which Weill spent his two years in France:

> A simple country house in a charming village outside Paris has become Weill's second home. Here everything breathes an air of serenity – the countryside, the little village, the house. Both the grounds and the architecture of the house itself are unusual. The high hall with its natural wood beams and large chimney remind one that the house was

> once a smithy. A wooden step leads from the hall to three bright, friendly rooms, simply furnished with a few beautiful pieces of old furniture.[29]

Here at Louveciennes Weill wrote the music for *Marie Galante*, a musical play based on a novel by Jacques Deval, composed a number of songs on French texts, *Der Kuhhandel* – a political operetta based on a libretto by Robert Vaubery and, in February 1934, completed the Second Symphony.

Marie Galante was first performed at the Théâtre de Paris in Paris on 2 December 1933. In mid-summer 1934 Weill and Lotte Lenya visited England for the première of *Der Kuhhandel* (temporarily entitled *Kingdom for a Cow*) at the Savoy Theatre in London on 28 June. While in London, Lotte Lenya also took part in performances of *The Seven Deadly Sins* and a version of the *Mahagonny Songspiel* at the Savoy. The Second Symphony received its first performance by the Concertgebouw Orchestra under Bruno Walter in Amsterdam on 11 October 1934. The performance received a cool reception and the work remained unpublished until 1966.

In the later summer of 1934 Weill was approached to write the score for a Biblical drama – *Der Weg der Verheissung (The Way of the Promise)* – by Franz Werfel. The work, the idea of which originated with Max Reinhardt, was to be a monumental pageant depicting the development and the fate of the Jewish people. Weill had long since moved away from his orthodox Jewish background and, for many years, had admitted only to being a humanist. Nonetheless, the persecution of the German Jews which he had witnessed, and from which he had suffered, forced him, as it did many others – including Schoenberg – to become more consciously aware of his Jewish ancestry. Weill accepted the commission and, turning to the Jewish music of his youth for his inspiration, worked on the piece from August 1934 until December 1935. The première, scheduled for early 1936, was to take place in New York after which the production would tour the United States. Weill had been invited to conduct the first performance and, in September 1935, he sailed for New York in order to prepare for the première. He was to return to Europe only once during the remaining fifteen years of his life, and then only very briefly.

Chapter 5
The American Years

The Weills sailed into New York on the S S Majestic on 10 September 1935. On arrival they booked in at the St Moritz Hotel, overlooking Central Park, and went to see a film:

> We were ardent readers of people like Hemingway and Scott Fitzgerald, and we saw all the movies. So when we arrived, we dropped our bags and went to Broadway into a movie. We saw *The Dark Angel* with Ronald Coleman and Vilma Blank. That was the first thing and from then on there was really nothing strange or unfamiliar.[1]

Weill had left Europe intending to stay in America for only a few months, until *Der Weg der Verheissung* was produced at the beginning of 1936. However, the work soon ran into trouble and even before rehearsals began, a series of crises had eaten up all the available money. Reinhardt and his designer Norman Bel Geddes (a man who, according to one writer 'despised anything less than ten feet tall'[2]) had visions of a spectacle of the most epic and lavish proportions, with a cast that included forty-three principal actors and scenic designs that at some points operated on three separate levels. One set, for example, was to show a contemporary synagogue on the lowest of the three levels, Moses in the wilderness on the central level and, at the top, a representation of the heavens, complete with angelic chorus.

In order to accommodate the production, the Manhattan Opera House, where the work was to be mounted, had to be radically modified. At an early stage in the preparation it had been decided that the orchestra pit would be needed as part of the stage area; the orchestra would, therefore, have to be moved. Even then the pit was not deep enough to contain the spectacular effects proposed by Reinhardt and Bel Geddes, and the decision was taken to deepen it by drilling down into the bedrock beneath. Unfortunately, the drill hit a spring – sending a spout of water some twenty-one feet (six metres) high into the auditorium – which then had to be capped before work could continue. With such set-backs it was not long before new financial backing was urgently needed. As rehearsals started and as crisis followed crisis, the date of the opening was postponed time and again until Weill found himself having to search for work in order to stay in the United States until the show was finally mounted.

Weill's music was not generally known by the American public at that time, and certainly did not enjoy the kind of reputation which it had in Europe. Of all his works only *The Threepenny Opera* had been staged in America before 1935 and that production, the first English language production of the work, had had a bad critical reception. Opening on 13 April 1933 at the Empire Theatre in New York *The Threepenny Opera* had run for a mere twelve performances. However, Weill's works were known to a number of important musicians and theatre people. George Gershwin, for example, was already an admirer of Weill's music and, a few weeks after Weill's arrival in the United States, had invited him to attend the dress rehearsal for the première of *Porgy and Bess* (which had its first night at the Alvin Theatre on 10 October 1935), while in December 1935 a New York concert of Weill's music was promoted by the influential League of Composers.

Many left-wing theatre groups, aware of Weill's European reputation, had given him a warm welcome and, early in 1936, the Group Theatre of New York commissioned a score for *Johnny Johnson*, a musical play by Paul Green, Professor of drama at the University of North Carolina and a former Pulitzer prize winner. An anti-militaristic satire, *Johnny Johnson* tells the story of a Schweyk-like figure who, involved against his will, manages to disrupt the war by spraying the entire allied High Command with laughing gas. Committed to a mental institution because of this insane act, he and his fellow inmates establish a League of World Republics and he is finally allowed to return to his home village where he devotes himself to selling non-martial toys.

It was the policy of the Group Theatre, a splinter group of the prestigious Theatre Guild, to spend the summer working at a summer camp, where its members could receive 'intensive training in the art of interpretation and ensemble playing'.[3] Weill spent the summer of 1936 at the Group Theatre's summer camp, lecturing and working on the score for Green's play. It was during this same period that he first met Elmer Rice, the dramatist whose Pulitzer prize winner *Street Scene* Weill had seen in Europe. Weill offered to write a score for the play but Rice thought it 'too early for a show of that sort' and the plan was temporarily abandoned.

Directed by Lee Strasberg, *Johnny Johnson* received its première at the Group Theatre's New York base on 44th Street on 19 November 1936, with a cast that included Lee J. Cobb, Elia Kazan and John Garfield. It was, according to Brook Atkinson, 'not very well acted by the Group Theatre, which seemed unable to master the form. The show was admired without being liked'.[4] It ran for sixty-eight performances.

Meanwhile, *Der Weg der Verheissung* was being subjected to yet further delays. The piece had been designed to arouse interest in the Jewish tradition and was to have been given as a charity performance with the proceeds going towards helping the persecuted Jews in Germany. However, it soon became clear that, given the scale of the production, the lengthy rehearsal period (the opening night was postponed ten times in all) and the escalating costs (which eventually rose to $540,000) – the show was unlikely to make any profit for anyone. In an attempt to save the piece, both the score and the play were subjected to savage cuts. Even then, when the mutilated version of *Der Weg der Verheissung*, now entitled *The Eternal Road*, finally opened at the Manhattan Opera House on 7 January 1937 the four-act play ran until three o'clock the following morning. During the weeks after the première yet more of Weill's score and Werfel's play was cut in order to reduce the, by now thoroughly mutilated, work to manageable proportions. The press, overwhelmed by Reinhardt's lavish production, gave the piece rave reviews and the show ran for 153 performances. Although it played to packed houses throughout and there was not a single empty seat for the whole run, it was a financial disaster and made a loss of $5,000.

By the summer of 1937 Weill had decided not only to remain in America but also to become an American citizen. This decision necessitated his leaving and re-entering the States, and, in order to fulfil these immigration requirements, he dutifully left New York for Canada in the late summer and crossed the border back into America on 27 August 1937.

At the same time Weill was again approached by Paul Green, the author of *Johnny Johnson*, about the possibility of his writing a score for *The Common Glory*, a piece commissioned by the government-sponsored Federal Theatre – a short-lived project set up in 1935, as part of the New Deal work-creation scheme, for the purpose of creating a national American theatre. Weill began but never completed the score.

A new, more hopeful, project was begun in March of the following year when Weill started work on a political satire about New York in the 1880s based on Washington Irving's book *Dietrich Knickerbocker's History of New York*. The idea for this piece, which became *Knickerbocker Holiday*, seems to have come from Weill, who saw the subject as a means of commenting upon the rise of Fascism in Europe. Maxwell Anderson, one of the leading American dramatists of the time, was asked to write the libretto. Weill had met and become friends with Anderson at a performance of Anderson's *Winterset* which the composer attended soon after his arrival in the States. Anderson agreed to write the text and the Playwrights' Company, a company recently founded by Anderson and four other writers as a means of producing their own plays without the help of commercial managements, agreed to mount the work in its first season. Anderson was to become Weill's closest collaborator during the remaining years of the composer's life.

In Anderson's play for *Knickerbocker Holiday* Washington Irving, having decided to write a history of Old New York, is transported from the early nineteenth-century to seventeenth-century New Amsterdam. Irving's arrival coincides with that of the new governor of New Amsterdam, Peter Stuyvesant. Adopting dictatorial methods of government, Stuyvesant gradually abolishes the freedom and liberties of the people, sentencing to jail any who protest. When the town is invaded by Indians, Brom Broeck, a protester with whose girl friend Stuyvesant is in love, escapes from jail and leads the fight against the attackers. Accused by Broeck of conspiring with the Indians, Stuyvesant sentences Broeck to death. Irving then intervenes and, reminding Stuyvesant of the way in which future generations will judge the action, wins a reprieve for Broeck.

The New York première of *Knickerbocker Holiday* took place at the Ethel Barrymore Theatre on 19 October 1938; the director was Joshua Logan, the conductor Maurice Abravanel, Weill's former pupil and the conductor of the first production of *The Seven Deadly Sins*. The star of the show, playing Peter Stuyvesant, was Walter

Huston for whom Weill wrote 'September Song', perhaps the most famous of his American numbers. According to Lotte Lenya, Weill decided to write this piece after hearing Huston sing on the radio one night: 'He was singing a famous patter song "I haven't got the Do Re Mi" and Kurt suddenly said, "You know, I'm going to write for him the most romantic song I can possibly write". From Walter's crackling voice Kurt heard something in the night.'[5]

Knickerbocker Holiday, the first of Weill's Broadway scores, was a considerable success (it ran for a respectable 168 performances) and, as the second piece to be staged by the Playwright's Company in its first season, it helped establish the new company as a viable concern. It was not, however, a 'smash hit' – Weill had to wait another three years, until the première of *Lady in the Dark*, for his first Broadway hit.

David Drew has suggested that Weill passed through some kind of personal crisis during the years 1939-40.[6] If this is so (and the fact that, as Drew has pointed out, *Lady in the Dark*, Weill's next Broadway show, inhabits a radically different world from that of his previous American works[7] lends weight to the suggestion) it may well have been a crisis occasioned by the course of events in Europe.

On 1 September 1939, following the annexation of Austria in March 1938, the Munich Agreement of September 1938 and the consequent annexation of Czechoslovakia in March 1939, Hitler began his invasion of Poland. The British and French declared war on 3 September 1939. The spring of 1940 saw the first of a series of German victories which led, in a little over two months, to the German domination of almost the whole of Western Europe. By June 1942 Norway, Denmark, France, Holland, Belgium and Luxembourg had fallen to the German army. Weill must have realized that, whatever the outcome of the war, the Germany and the Europe that he had known had disappeared for ever.

For whatever reason, Weill wrote few substantial works in the two years that followed *Knickerbocker Holiday*. Two large-scale projects – a folk-opera on the subject of Davy Crockett with a libretto by Charles Allen and a musical play entitled *Ulysses Africanus* with Maxwell Anderson – were begun and abandoned. The only deeply personal work of this period is the short cantata *Magna Carta* (also on an Anderson text) which Weill wrote at the beginning of 1940 and which received its first performance on the CBS 'Pursuit of Happiness' programme on 4 February that year. Otherwise, the works of this two-year period consist of routine pieces written to fulfil the various commissions which Weill's growing reputation now attracted: two film scores (one for the *Goldwyn Follies*, an MGM spectacular directed by George Marshall, and one for *You and Me*, a film directed by Fritz Lang), the incidental music to *Madam Will you Walk*, a play by Sidney Howard, and a musical pageant *Railroads on Parade*, with a text by Edward Hungerford, written for the New York World Exhibition and given its première on 30 April 1939. As a result of these commissions Weill was able to buy the house, with large grounds and a private brook, at New City, Rockville County, in which he lived for the rest of his life.

In 1940 Weill began work with Moss Hart and Ira Gershwin on a new musical, *Lady in the Dark*. For Hart it was the first play he had written without the collaboration of his usual partner George S Kaufmann; for Gershwin it was the first piece to be written after the death of his brother George. The story of *Lady in the Dark* deals with the psychological problems and fantasies of the lady editor of a successful fashion magazine. Troubled by recurring dreams, which feature the four men in her life, and by the attempts to recapture a melody from her childhood, the heroine finally relates her dreams to a psychoanalyst and is able to recognize her love for one of the men.

Gershwin, who lived in California, moved up to New York and for four months during the hot summer of 1940 the three men worked – in New York during the week and at Hart's summer home in Bucks County at the week-ends – on the new piece. Gershwin then returned home and Weill retired to his house in New York State to orchestrate the music.

With such an experienced and skilful team of writers, with a cast that included Gertrude Lawrence (in what proved to be one of her most memorable rôles) and the young Danny Kaye, and with lavish production numbers elaborately mounted on the revolving stage, the show could hardly fail to be a success. *Lady in the Dark* had its preview in Boston and opened at the Alvin Theatre in New York on 23 January 1941. The show ran for two seasons, with a total of 467 performances in New York and then moved to Los Angeles in the autumn of 1943.

In 1944 Paramount, who had paid $300,000 for the rights – the highest sum Hollywood had ever paid for a Broadway musical – made *Lady in the Dark* into a film starring Ginger Rodgers and Ray Milland and directed by Mitchell Leisen.

In December 1941, following the Japanese attack on Pearl Harbor,

America entered the war, and from January 1942 to May 1943 – while *Lady in the Dark* was drawing enormous audiences to the Alvin Theatre – Weill devoted himself to helping organize lunch-time shows for factory workers.

Modelled on the British ENSA entertainments, these lunch-time shows, which came to be called the 'Lunchtime Follies', were simply mounted on a small platform equipped only with a piano and a couple of microphones. Originally lasting for about half-an-hour, the shows were reduced to twenty minutes as the war advanced and the lunch-time breaks were shortened. The show included a mixture of songs, dance numbers, sketches (the first show also presented a new sketch entitled 'The Man who came to Russia' by Kaufmann and Hart) and, usually, one serious item about the war. One such, frequently performed, serious item was Maxwell Anderson's dramatization of Commander Shea's letters to his son.

The 'Lunchtime Follies' were organized by Weill, Moss Hart, the composer Harald Rome and Kermit Bloomgarten (the leader of the Group Theatre) from a small office above the Lyceum Theatre. Delighted at being able to help the war effort, Weill took particular pleasure in the immediacy of the audience contact which these shows afforded; the opening of the first show he later described as 'one of the most exciting moments in my theatrical life'.[8] Characteristically, Weill saw these popular lunch-time entertainments as suggesting new directions in which theatre might move in peacetime.

During 1942 Weill also composed a number of other patriotic pieces: a ballad for baritone and chorus, on a text by Archibald MacLeish, entitled *Song of the Free*; *Recitations*, a melodrama for speaker and orchestra which employed patriotic themes and texts drawn from poems by Walt Whitman; and four *Walt Whitman Songs* for baritone and orchestra. He also set two German texts by Mehring and by Brecht which he and Lotte Lenya performed on a Voice of America broadcast in support of the war effort.

Many of Weill's Berlin friends were living in the United States during the war and, in 1942 and 1943, a number of them made attempts to revive the collaboration with Brecht who was then living in California. In autumn 1942 Brecht, who had been working in Hollywood on Fritz Lang's *Hangmen also Die*, paid a four-month visit to New York to see Erwin Piscator who was planning to produce a version of Brecht's *The Private Life of the Master Race* in the spring of 1943. Weill and Brecht met on 1 October 1942, their first meeting since 1935 when Weill had just arrived in America. Earlier in 1942 T. W. Adorno had attempted to interest Brecht and Weill in doing a production of *The Threepenny Opera* but the plan had been abandoned. In early 1943 Aufricht, the man who had commissioned *The Threepenny Opera*, tried to bring Brecht and Weill together again to write a musical based on Jaroslav Hašek's *The Good Soldier Schweyk*. Again the plan came to nothing. The reason for this was that apparently Piscator was also engaged on an adaptation of the Schweyk story and Weill seems to have decided to abandon the project rather than risk widening the already serious rift between Piscator and Brecht.[9] Brecht continued to work on the adaptation by himself and it eventually became the play *Schweyk in the Second World War*. A further plan, for Weill to write the incidental music for Brecht's *The Good Woman of Setzuan*, was also discussed and abandoned.

Weill's involvement with the 'Lunchtime Follies' ended in May 1943 and he spent the summer of that year working on a new musical comedy called *One Touch of Venus*, with a text by S J Perelman and lyrics by Ogden Nash. The rather absurd plot of the work concerned a newly discovered statue of Venus which, displayed in a museum, comes to life and falls in love with a naive barber who chances to visit the museum. Having won the young man, and having lured him away from his girl friend, the goddess realizes that she cannot change herself into a mortal and turns back into stone. The work ends with the arrival of a new girl who is identical to the statue of Venus.

Continuing the atmosphere of the war-time shows, *One Touch of Venus*, with its light, witty score and its musical and verbal parodies, became Weill's longest-running Broadway show. Opening at the Imperial Theatre on 7 October 1943, *One Touch of Venus* ran for 567 performances. The conductor was, again, Maurice Abravanel; the director Elia Kazan. The star of the show, appearing in her first starring Broadway part in a rôle which had originally been intended for Dietrich, was Mary Martin, the future star of *South Pacific* and *The Sound of Music*.

Reviewing the show for the November issue of *Modern Music*, Elliot Carter offered some perceptive observations on both the strengths and weaknesses of Weill's Broadway work in general:

> Kurt Weill's new score for *One Touch of Venus*, coming after last year's *Lady in the Dark*, reveals his mastery of Broadway technique. Apparently he can turn out one success after another with a sure hand. Weill, who orchestrates and

> arranges his own work, whose flair for discovering and using the stylistic earmarks of popular music is remarkable, has finally made himself at home in America. Where in pre-Hitler days his music underlined the bold and disillusioned bitterness of economic injustice, now, reflecting his new environment and the New York audiences to which he appeals, his social scene has shrunk to the bedroom and he has become the composer of 'sophisticated' scores.
>
> The present one represents quite a piece of research into the phases of American love-life expressed in popular music – the barber-shop ballad, the bar-room song dripping with bloody murder, the serious and comic parodies of Cole Porter, an uproarious mock-patriotic 'Way Out West in Jersey' in the best college spirit style. Even the orchestration, with its numerous piano solos in boogie-woogie and other jazz styles, constantly recalls night-club atmosphere. Traces of the mordant composer of *Die Dreigroschenoper* and *Mahagonny* occur rarely and only in places where Weill is not trying to make an impression. Compared to his other American shows, the music is neither as ingenious and as striking as *Johnny Johnson*, nor as forced as his made-to-order jobs for *The Eternal Road* and the railroad show at the World's Fair. But in the atmosphere of Broadway, where so much music is unconvincing and dead, Weill's workmanlike care and his refined sense of style make up for whatever spontaneity and freshness his music lacks.[10]

One Touch of Venus, Weill's greatest Broadway success, was followed by the greatest disaster of his American career, the two-act operetta *The Firebrand of Florence* which took as its unlikely subject an episode from the life of Benvenuto Cellini. Cellini is suspected of having played a part in a conspiracy but he manages to convince the Duke of his innocence, thus winning the hand of his beloved Angela. The story is based on a book by Edwin J Meyer which had already formed the basis of a moderately successful 1924 musical, and with lyrics by Ira Gershwin, *The Firebrand of Florence* opened at the Alvin Theatre on 22 March 1945 – a fortnight before the end of the war – and ran for only forty-three performances.

David Drew sees *The Firebrand of Florence* as marking a real crisis in Weill's creative life and has described what he calls the 'crushing reception' of the work as being the point at which Weill was 'finally defeated'.[11] Certainly the period following *The Firebrand of Florence* saw another radical shift in Weill's musical style and in the final years of his life he deliberately abandoned the slicker techniques and glossy style of the Broadway musical to cultivate a simpler, more consciously American folk style. The next work which Weill wrote was a score for the film *Where Do We Go from Here*, but the first fruits of the effects which *The Firebrand of Florence* had on him appear in the one-act folk opera *Down in the Valley* which he wrote in September 1945.

Deliberately simple in both its musical and dramatic style *Down in the Valley* employs the characteristics of the American square-dance, barn-dance, folksong and church music to tell the story of Brack Weaver who, condemned to death, escapes from prison to be reunited with his girl friend. *Down in the Valley* was intended to be the first of a series of folk operas commissioned by commercial radio. In the event, the scheme collapsed and, in 1948, Weill and Arnold Sundgaard, the author of the text, rewrote the piece as an opera for performance by 'non-professional groups'. The work had its première in this form on 14 July 1948 at the University of Indiana campus at Bloomington.

Another folk work, the Broadway opera *Street Scene*, was composed in 1946. Based on Elmer Rice's 1929 Pulitzer Prize-winning play, *Street Scene* is set in front of an East Side tenement in New York City. The main story line of the work concerns an affair between Mrs Maurrant, one of the tenants, and the milkman. When, towards the end of the opera, Mrs Maurrant's husband learns of the affair he shoots his wife and her lover and is captured by the police. More important than this story, however, is the general picture of tenement life which the work attempts to convey, of the routines, the pastimes and the hopes, fears and dreams of those who occupy the building. Weill had first approached Rice about the possibility of setting *Street Scene* during a rehearsal for *Johnny Johnson*. Now he suggested the idea again:

> On a hot summer day in 1945, as we were leaving a Dramatists' Guild meeting together, we started talking about *Street Scene* again and decided that now was the time to do it. The Broadway musical scene had changed quite a bit in the ten years since we had first discussed the plan. Broadway composers had become more 'book conscious'. Opera was now a popular entertainment; the public had become interested in singing.

> Before the second drink arrived (we were planted in a cool bar by this time) Elmer and I had made up our minds to go ahead with *Street Scene*. We decided to do it as a musical version of the play, to cast it entirely with singers, so that the emotional climaxes could be expressed in music, and to use spoken dialogue to further the realistic action. In discussing the problem of lyrics for a show in which music had to grow out of the characters, we decided that the lyrics should attempt to lift the everyday language of the people into a simple unsophisticated poetry. We choose Langston Hughes for the job.[12]

The backers of the project were far from enthusiastic and were not encouraged by the try-out in Philadelphia, which Lotte Lenya has described as having been 'a disaster'. 'There were, maybe, 250 people in the audience and next door *Finian's Rainbow* was playing to standing room only.'[13] Billy Rose, the producer, attempted to persuade Weill to shorten some of the numbers and to make the operatic elements less important: 'Right after the show opens Mrs Maurrant sings an aria that takes perhaps eight or ten minutes. When he heard it, Billy Rose came to Kurt and said, 'Kurt, it's impossible. You have to shorten it – nobody will listen.' Kurt was very quiet and said to Billy: 'If that aria doesn't work then I haven't written the opera I wanted to write. I won't change a note.'[14] The backers were particularly worried about its being called an 'opera' ('the word opera frightened everybody on Broadway', remembers Lotte Lenya) and, when the show opened at the Adelphi Theatre on 9 January 1947, it bore the subtitle 'a dramatic musical'. Few critics were misled by this attempted disguise; Olin Downes, the critic of the *New York Times*, for example, unequivocally described it as an 'opera' and called the work 'the most important step towards significantly American opera yet encountered in musical theatre.'[15] Weill himself regarded the piece as having a special place in his output and said, 'Not until *Street Scene* did I achieve a real blending of drama and music in which the singing continues naturally when the speaking stops.'[16] *Street Scene* was not the hit of the season. *Finian's Rainbow*, which opened in New York on the night after *Street Scene*, ran for 725 performances and *Brigadoon*, opening two months later, for 581. Nevertheless *Street Scene* ran for 148 performances – a respectable number for an opera. Writing about Weill some two years after the première, Hans Heinsheimer chose to refer to *Street Scene* as one of the two American works his readers were likely to remember. By that time Weill was, said Heinsheimer,

> probably the most successful of the many European composers who came to the United States in the last decade. Weill is the composer of *Lady in the Dark* and *Street Scene*; he is a distinguished member of the Playwrights' Company . . . when you want to see him he has first to consult a calendar and will then ask you to be his guest for lunch at the Oak Room of the Plaza Hotel on the second Friday of next month 'unless I call you – I might have to go to Hollywood'.[17]

In June and July 1947 Weill went to Palestine to see his parents, visiting England, France, Switzerland and, for a few days only, Germany *en route*. It was his only visit to Europe in the fifteen years between his arrival in America and his death in 1950.

Returning to America at the end of July, he began work immediately on a new piece, originally called *A Dish for the Gods* and eventually entitled *Love Life*. The six episodes of *Love Life* were to depict the gradual erosion of the institution of marriage by presenting the different stages in the breakdown of a single marriage spread over some 150 years. Beginning in 1791 with a young, happily married couple, the various episodes gradually move forward in time towards, in the second act, the date at which the work was first performed, and show the increasing stress, cynicism and bitterness to which the relationship between the couple is subjected and which, eventually, leads to the final breakdown of the marriage. The book and the songs were by Alan Jay Lerner, the author of *Brigadoon* who was later to write *Paint Your Wagon* and *My Fair Lady*. *Love Life*, Weill's most ambitious Broadway show, opened at the 46th Street Theatre on 17 October 1948. The director was Elia Kazan. Unfortunately, the run of the piece was seriously affected, as were all the other shows being played at the time, by a prolonged ASCAP strike and it had only 258 performances.

For his last completed Broadway work Weill returned to Maxwell Anderson, the writer of his earliest Broadway musicals, and to the kind of social themes that had dominated Weill's earlier works but had disappeared in his slicker commercial pieces. Described as 'a musical tragedy', *Lost in the Stars* was based on Alan Paton's novel *Cry the Beloved Country* and tells the story of a rural black preacher,

Stephen Kumodo, and his wife who go to Johannesburg in search of their son Absalom. When discovered, the son is under arrest for his involvement in a robbery, in the course of which a young white man was killed. Of those implicated, Absalom alone confesses his guilt in court and is sentenced to death. Moved by the honesty of Absalom's confession, the father of the dead youth approaches Kumodo and some kind of reconciliation is affected between the two fathers and the two races.

Directed by Rouben Mamoulian and presented by the Playwrights' Company, the work opened on 30 October 1949 at the Music Box Theatre in New York. For a work with a tragic story and a serious social message it had a considerable success and ran for 273 performances. Nonetheless it received a mixed critical reception, the *New York Times* finding it 'not altogether successful';[18] the *Herald Tribune* describing it as 'magnificent . . . moving to its climax inexorably with a tremendous crescendo';[19] while the *New Yorker* critic, who thought that the 'tragedy never rises above the level of a melodramatic device', admitted to being 'one of a small, wayward minority'.[20]

The effect which it had upon the public can perhaps be best judged from a review by Henry Hewes (who saw the original production) of the 1972 revival at the J F Kennedy Centre for the Performing Arts. He described how he and other 'old timers' were both moved by the performance of 'the season's best and most thrilling musical' and also 'moved by the memory of how they had felt in 1949'.[21]

At the end of 1949 Weill was full of plans for future projects including a musical play of Twain's *Huckleberry Finn* on which he and Maxwell Anderson began work in December. Although Weill completed five songs the score was never finished, for at the end of March 1950 he had a heart attack and was taken to the Flowers Hospital in New York where he died on 3 April. He was buried in Haverstraw Cemetery overlooking the Hudson River on 5 April 1950.

Part Two
Assessing the Music

Chapter 6
The Early Instrumental and Vocal Music

The Italian composer Luigi Dallapiccola has described an occasion, in March 1942, when the name of Kurt Weill cropped up during the course of a conversation between himself and Anton Webern. The usually mild-mannered Webern reacted violently:

> Webern suddenly explodes. He points his finger at me (although I had not been the one who introduced the name of the composer he disliked) and asks me: 'What do you find of our great Middle-European tradition in such a composer – that tradition which includes the names of Schubert, Brahms, Wolff, Mahler, Schoenberg, Berg and myself?'[1]

In the diary in which he recorded the event, Dallapiccola admits to having been surprised by the fact that Webern saw his own music as part of the Middle-European tradition; to Webern, observed Dallapiccola, it was not 'a question of aesthetics and of taste that separated him from Kurt Weill, but rather the fact that Weill had refused the Middle-European tradition.'[2] It is indicative of the misunderstanding which Weill's music suffered in his lifetime, and has continued to suffer since, that Dallapiccola did not, for one moment, question Webern's assumption that Weill had broken with 'Middle-European tradition'.

In fact, both Webern and Weill grew up and developed their musical styles within the same Middle-European tradition and were deeply influenced by the same late romantic, hyper-expressive branch of that tradition. Weill's writings (such as the articles in which he describes how many of his ideas on music theatre sprang from his study of the works of Mozart, Beethoven, Weber and Bach) reveal the extent to which he himself regarded even the apparently iconoclastic, jazz-influenced work of the late 1920s and 1930s (presumably the works against which Webern's outburst was directed) as belonging to that same Austro-German tradition.

Much of Weill's earliest music remains unavailable. However, from what is available it is clear that the most important influences on these early works were Mahler, Schoenberg, Strauss, Schreker (with whom Weill had once thought of studying) and the other late romantic composers; influences of the kind which, at a time when expressionism dominated German music as well as the visual and literary arts, one might expect to find in the music of any talented young composer eager to become acquainted with and to assimilate the newest and most advanced ideas of the day.

Indebted to Mahler in its emotional atmosphere, to Schoenberg in its formal design and to both these composers – and others, such as Strauss and Liszt – in its typically German concern with thematic transformation and motivic integration, the First Symphony of 1921 clearly demonstrates Weill's musical origins in the post-Wagnerian German tradition.

Formally the First Symphony attempts to weld the usually distinct three or four movements of a traditional symphony into a single large-scale structure. Schoenberg had attempted such integrated single-movement structures in his First Quartet and First Chamber Symphony by spreading the different sections of the traditional sonata-form movement throughout the work in such a way that the sonata exposition and first reprise might be separated by the slow movement; the first reprise and development sections by a scherzo and the development and recapitulation by an allegro Finale. The twenty-one-year-old Weill certainly knew these works, just as the eighteen-year-old Weill had, apparently, known Schoenberg's *Pelleas und Melisande* when, as a pupil at the Hochschüle, he had composed the Rilke tone poem.[3] Much of the instrumentation of the First Symphony, the chords built of perfect fourths which open the piece and the chains of fourths which form the melody of the *Sehr wuchtig* section, are immediately reminiscent of Schoenberg's First Chamber Symphony. Influenced by the design of the Chamber Symphony and similar works of Schoenberg, Weill also attempts an ingenious, if not entirely successful, formal structure in which the three movements, linked by recurring motifs, themes and occasionally sections, are juxtaposed to form a single span.

The first movement proper is preceded by an introduction in which are stated the two most important themes of the work (‘a’ and ‘b’ in Ex 1 below, and a variant of ‘b’, the cell ‘b^1’) which give rise to other important thematic ideas. These themes occur constantly throughout the work and are subjected to numerous transformations. The first movement itself begins with a relatively traditional sonata exposition (the themes of the two subject groups being derived from, or including, those of Ex 1). The usual development section, however, is replaced by two episodes while the recapitulation is confined to a reprise of the first subject group and a reprise of the first of the two central episodes. The other sections of the movement are then recapitulated during the course of the other two movements, the second of the two episodes appearing in the middle of the *Andante Religioso* second movement and the second subject group, followed by a re-statement of the introduction to the first movement, reappearing at the end of the third and final movement; the whole work is bound together by the appearance of diminutions, augmentations, inversions and other transformations of the themes of Ex 1.

The influence of Schoenberg, which is so strong a feature of the First Symphony, appeared early in Weill’s output and survived, in some form, throughout his student years; it is an influence that is still faintly discernible in the Violin Concerto of 1924 and in the pre-Brecht operas. Thereafter, it disappeared from Weill’s music, although Weill himself remained an ardent admirer of Schoenberg, recognizing both his historical significance and his courage in facing the consequences of post-Wagnerian chromaticism. *Pierrot Lunaire* Weill regarded as a 'work that has brought about a new epoch in music history'[4] and, in two essays written in 1926, he described Schoenberg as 'the purest, most lofty-minded artistic personality and the greatest intellect of present-day life . . . he is the only one who has unflinchingly held fast to the pursuit of his goal. His full significance for the musical public will probably only become clear after another decade.'[5] He wrote an equally generous review of Berg's *Wozzeck*, describing its première in December 1925 as 'the greatest event in Berlin's musical life for many years'.[6]

While the influence of Schoenberg's music gradually waned, that of Mahler never disappeared from Weill's work. On a technical level the lasting influence of Mahler can be seen in Weill's orchestration, in which the simultaneous use of strongly differentiated timbres (the contrasting, rather than the blending, of colours within a small group of instruments) in the latter European pieces springs from the use of 'opposing timbres' and the 'soloistic, almost chamber music-like' handling of the orchestra in Mahler's works; Weill himself commented on these features in his review of a performance of Mahler's Ninth Symphony,[7] On an expressive level Mahler's influence remains not only in those gestures and passages that have a typically late romantic emotional intensity (and such passages appear even in Weill's works with Brecht) but, more importantly, in Weill's later use of 'popular' music as a means of expressing a moral attitude. Weill's gradual development of a simpler, more accessible musical language in the late 1920s will be discussed in the following chapter, but it is worth pointing out, while considering Weill's musical roots, the extent to which Mahler, as the first composer deliberately to exploit the emotional associations of 'cheap' popular music, anticipated a technique that was to become the basis of Weill's later style. It is perhaps more than a coincidence that while Weill's early music is firmly Teutonic in inspiration and reveals nothing of his Jewish musical ancestry (indeed *Der Weg der Verheissung*, and a few occasional pieces written when Weill had fled his native country, are the only works in which he seems to have consciously exploited his Jewish musical background) it is, like that of his fellow Jews Mahler and Schoenberg, deeply concerned with moral and religious themes. The religious element in the programme which lies behind the First Symphony is clearly indicated by its subtitle 'A People's Awakening to God'. David Drew has described the extent to which the *Divertimento* (with its 'feeling of religious fear' of the 'vengeful Jehovah of the old Testament')[8] and the *Sinfonia Sacra* continue this religious preoccupation. The purely religious aspects of Weill's First Symphony were to disappear from his music within a few years of the work's completion; the moral and social concerns which are also implicit in the Symphony's full subtitle were to be a constant preoccupation of his work.

Unlike Webern, who, as a pupil of Schoenberg, was brought up only in the mainstream of the Austro-German tradition, Weill was also affected by influences outside this Middle-European tradition. Undoubtedly the most important of these influences was that of his teacher Ferruccio Busoni, whose ideas brought about a radical change in Weill's already-formed musical style. 'We young musicians', wrote Weill in a tribute to his teacher, 'were filled with new ideas and new hopes but we could not find the form for our content. We had burst the chains but we could do nothing with the freedom we had won . . . then Busoni came to Berlin.'[9]

Busoni's influence on Weill's view of music theatre will be discussed in the following chapter but many of Busoni's ideas, in particular his belief in the possibility of employing some kind of expanded tonality rather than turning to atonality and his opposition to the highly emotional atmosphere of the German post-Wagnerian composers, had a deep effect on Weill. Busoni is said to have loathed Wagner and all that he stood for to such an extent that he 'could hardly bring himself to write down the name'.[10] Busoni had a particular horror of the lush textures of Wagner's music and of the eroticism of Wagner and the post-Wagnerian composers; Wagner, he declared, had 'ruined music with his lasciviousness'[11] while the openly erotic operas of a composer such as Schreker, whose *Die Gezeichneten* he saw in 1921, 'aroused in him an almost moral indignation'.[12]

In challenging the hyper-emotionalism of the expressionist composers Busoni advocated a cool, objective music and a classicism based upon what he described as 'the masterly sifting and exploration of all the achievements of past experiments and their embodiment in fixed and beautiful forms.'[13]

Busoni's 'young classicism' was in accord with a general musical trend towards the exploitation of the styles, figurations and forms of earlier music. This trend, which has become known as neo-classicism (although the models to which its adherent turned were more frequently those of the baroque than those of the eighteenth century) had both purely musical and social causes.

During the course of the nineteenth century, the gradual extension of the time span over which a piece operated, coupled with the growing complexity of the harmonic and melodic language, had undermined the long-term organizational function of tonality which had been a feature of the music of the classical period. By the early years of the twentieth century, the further development of post-Wagnerian chromaticism and the gradual appearance of music in which tonal criteria no longer operated, had led to a point at which the tonal system – the system which had been the basis of Western musical thought and expression for over three hundred years – seemed about to collapse. Faced with this prospect, many composers turned back to the music of the past in an attempt both to find something stable to which they could cling and to find a way out of the predicament. Busoni's call for a 'sifting' of the achievements of the past and his advocacy of some kind of 'expanded' tonality, as opposed to atonality, are characteristic manifestations of the attitude of those composers who rejected Schoenberg's more radical solution to the problem. But neo-classicism was not simply a negative reaction to the musical crisis which seemed imminent; it was also one aspect of that positive rejection of the self-contemplation, the inturned, subjective emotionalism of the expressionists which characterized much art after the First World War and which has been discussed in general terms in Chapter Two.

Under Busoni, Weill turned away from the extreme expressionistic style of his earlier atonal works and towards the cooler, more objective idiom advocated by his teacher – a neo-classical idiom characterized by clearer melodic and rhythmic patterns, more lucid instrumental textures and a more rigorous and cleaner contrapuntal style. The sudden neo-classical interest in strict 'Bachian' contrapuntal thought and the use of Bach-like figurations, is particularly striking in the works which Weill wrote during his student years, many of which have movements based on specifically baroque forms. Thus, the String Quartet op 8 has a Chorale Fantasia as its last movement, the *Divertimento* a Chorale Prelude and the *Sinfonia Sacra* a Passacaglia.

Weill's change of style is immediately apparent if one compares the First Symphony of 1921 with the music of *Der Zaubernacht* and the orchestral *Quodlibet* which Weill drew from the ballet, or with the charming *Frauentanz* of 1923: the atonal emotional language of the Symphony has given way to an overtly neo-classical tonal idiom, the expressionistic gestures and complex rhythmic patterns to simple melodic and jaunty rhythmic figures, the complex, multi-layered orchestral thought to simple textures and unmixed timbres (favouring wind and brass) which look forward to the later Weill.

In opposing the Germanic, late-romantic tradition in which Weill had been brought up, and in which he had first established some kind of musical identity, Busoni created within Weill a creative conflict which took many years to resolve. The extent to which this stylistic conflict is apparent in the works which Weill wrote during the mid- and early 1920s varies from piece to piece – the *Quodlibet* and the *Frauentanz*, for example, are fairly assured works in the new neo-classical style; it is, nevertheless, a conflict that runs, in varying degrees, throughout much of Weill's music of this period. The effects of the conflict are, for example, clearly apparent even in the Violin Concerto of 1924, written after the *Quodlibet* and the *Frauentanz*, when Weill was already involved in planning *The Protagonist*, the work which was to mark his almost total abandonment of instrumental music.

Though separated into three distinct movements (the second of which is itself subdivided into three 'character pieces') the Violin Concerto seems more diffuse, less of a total entity than did the First Symphony, with its complex single-span structure. Thematically undistinguished and incessantly 'busy', the generation of activity seems in the Violin Concerto (as in much neo-classical music) to have become an end in itself and a substitute for real ideas. The confidence of the First Symphony has disappeared but the old style has not been replaced by anything which seems to elicit the same degree of assurance. Instead of the unified musical language of the earlier work, one finds a heterogeneous collection of stylistic influences, remnants of the influence of Schoenberg and Mahler rubbing shoulders with that of Busoni, Stravinsky and Hindemith. It is perhaps symbolic of this inner conflict that the rather dry and arid String Quartet op 8 should attempt to draw into its neo-classical world material from the First Symphony.

If such pieces as the Violin Concerto and the Quartet op 8 seem characterless when compared to the First Symphony one must remember that these pieces, like all Weill's instrumental music with the sole exception of the Second Symphony, are the works of a young immature composer whose musical ideas have been overturned at a crucial stage of his development. Perhaps the stylistic conflict which Busoni precipitated in Weill's music mirrored a deeper conflict between the romantic and anti-romantic elements within the character of Weill himself. At any rate, Weill never fully renounced the subjective, late romantic expressionist influences which had formed the style of his earliest music or fully embraced the objective neo-classical style advocated by his teacher. Instead, the objective and subjective elements of the two styles – and of Weill's own nature – produced a conflict which was to become the creative impulse behind, and is still one of the chief fascinations of, his mature musical style.

The only purely instrumental work of Weill's mature years, the Second Symphony of 1933-4, is a graphic demonstration of the extent to which the new musical language, which he forged in the stage works which followed *The Protagonist*, grew out of the conflicting demands of neo-classicism and expressionism. Although it employs no single cyclic theme throughout, the Second, like the First Symphony, makes considerable use of Lisztian thematic transformations. Thus, the trumpet theme which closes the introduction to the first movement (Ex 2a) is transformed into the second movement theme shown in Ex 2b, while another second movement theme (Ex 2c) reappears, in turn, as a jaunty third movement figuration (Ex 2d). Similarly, the coda of the third movement has its origins in the melodic idea which opens the second movement (Ex 2e and f).

Ex 2

Such devices for ensuring the thematic unity of the piece, the Mahlerian march with which the work opens, and the closely integrated motivic relationships which spring from this opening figuration, are immediately reminiscent of the techniques of the late romantic composers. In the Second Symphony, however, such thematic and motivic relationships operate within a formal design that is much more traditional and much clearer than that of the First Symphony. The complications that appear – such as the disassociation of the return to the home key and the traditionally simultaneous return to the original material in the first movement, or the Haydnesque introduction of the first movement coda long before its allotted place[14] – operate within the outlines of the traditional symphonic structure.

Above all the Second Symphony, with its Mendelssohnian finale and its Mahlerian rhythms and instrumental effects (such as the trombone solo in the second movement) reveals, far more clearly than do the stage and the vocal works of the same period, the extent to which Weill's mature 'popular' language has its roots in that German tradition the influence of which is so clearly seen in his early instrumental music.

Chapter 7
The European Dramatic and Vocal Works

The première of *The Protagonist* in March 1926 established Weill, almost overnight, as one of the leading theatre composers of the day. After *The Protagonist* the twenty-six-year-old Weill only once, with the Second Symphony, returned to purely instrumental composition; the rest of his life was to be entirely devoted to the composition of either stage works or of vocal works, many of which had strong dramatic associations.

Weill's characteristic, and highly individual, approach to the relationship between music and text and the beginnings of that deliberately simpler musical style that is a feature of his best known music can already be seen in *The Protagonist* and the works which immediately followed it. It is not suprising, perhaps, that the first signs of this simpler style should coincide with the beginnings of Weill's career as a theatre composer: music that is effective in the theatre tends to employ broader, less intricate, gestures and to operate over a larger time span than music conceived for the concert hall. In Weill's case, however, the search for a simpler style was to lead, not to a modification of the style employed in his earlier music, but to a radically different kind of music.

Since this new, simpler and more popular style first came to fruition in the *Mahagonny Songspiel* and *The Threepenny Opera* – that is, in the first of the works which Weill wrote in collaboration with Brecht – it is frequently assumed that the change in style was entirely due to Brecht's influence. This assumption is encouraged by a number of coincidental factors: by the fact that the scores of many of Weill's works have for long been unobtainable (some of them, including some of the key works in Weill's development, having been either lost

Kurt Weill and Lotte Lenya at their home in New City, Rockville County, 1942

Querida

ABOVE *Franz Werfel, the author, Max Reinhardt, the director, and Weill, during the preparations of* The Eternal Road, *New York 1935-36* BELOW *The Group Theatre's production of* Johnny Johnson, *directed by Lee Strasberg, November 1936. Morris Carnovsky (centre) as the Psychiatrist and Russell Collins (right) as Johnny Johnson* ABOVE LEFT *The Princesse Edmonde de Polignac, who was one of the great patrons of new music during the first half of the twentieth century and who commissioned Weill's Second Symphony* BELOW LEFT *Scene from the première of* Marie Galante *at the Théâtre de Paris, December 1933*

ABOVE *A production still from the* The Eternal Road. *The photograph gives some idea of the size of the spectacular multi-level set created for Reinhardt's lavish production* OPPOSITE ABOVE LEFT *The opening of* The Eternal Road. *A cartoon by B. F. Doblin for the New York Post of January 8th 1937 showing Werfel and Weill (top), Norman Bel Geddes (the designer), Max Reinhardt and Meyer Weisgall (producer)* OPPOSITE ABOVE RIGHT *Weill with Maxwell Anderson; the writer of* Knickerbocker Holiday *and* Lost in the Stars, *New York 1949* OPPOSITE BELOW *Walter Huston as Peter Stuyvesant in the original production of* Knickerbocker Holiday *at the Ethel Barrymore Theatre, New York 1938*

LAUNCHING "THE ETERNAL ROAD"

ABOVE *Gertrude Lawrence and Victor Mature in the 'Circus Dream' sequence of* Lady in the Dark. *The show ran for two years on Broadway before transferring to Los Angeles* ABOVE RIGHT *Weill and Agnes de Mille, the choreographer, at a rehearsal of* One Touch of Venus, *1943* BELOW RIGHT *Weill and his parents Albert and Emma Weill at Nahariya, Palestine, in the summer of 1947, looking at the newly published score of Weill's* Street Scene

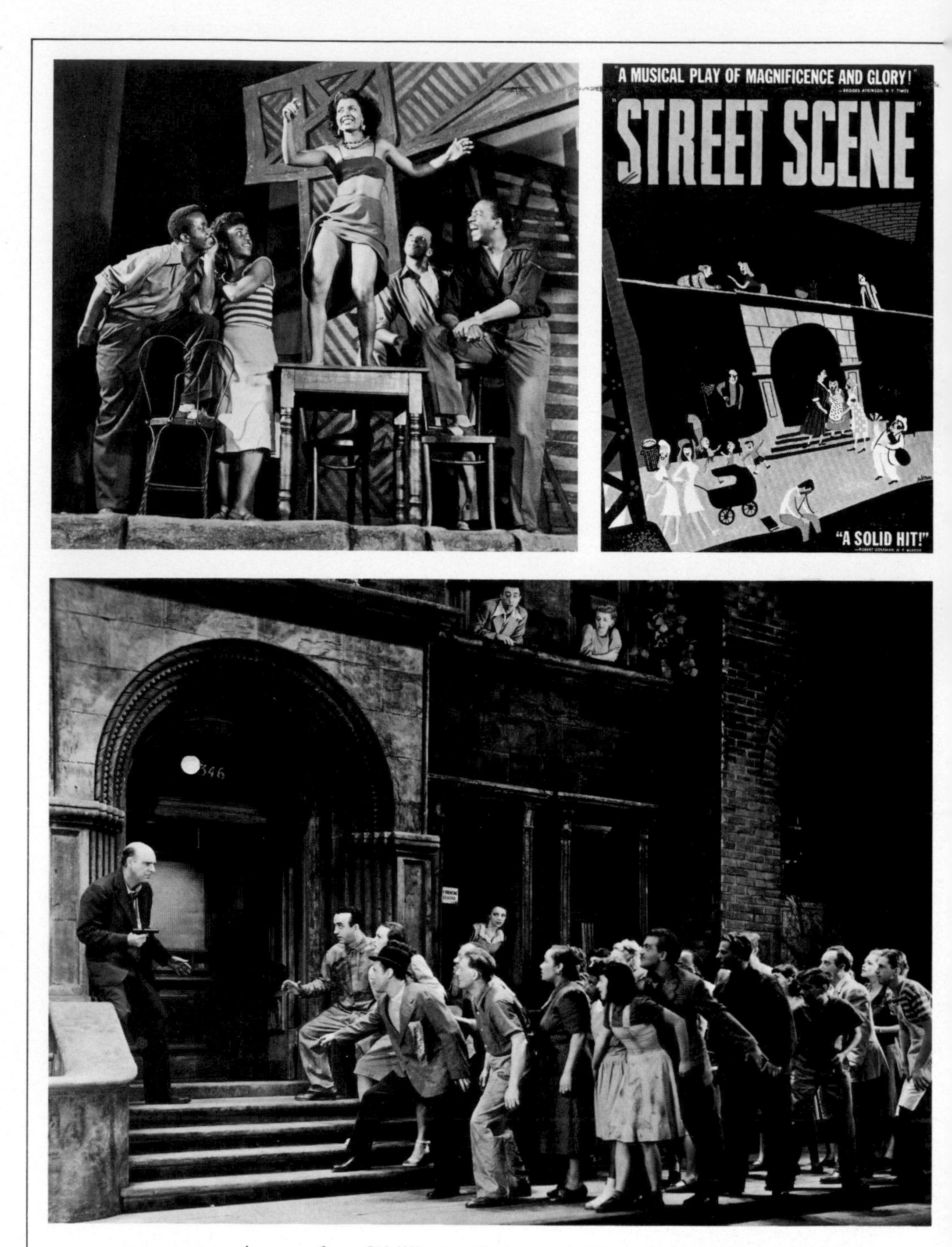

TOP LEFT *A scene from Weill's 'musical tragedy'* Lost in the Stars, *his last completed work. From left to right: William Greaves, Gloria Smith, Sheila Guyse, Lavern French and Van Prince* TOP RIGHT *Playbill from the original production of* Street Scene *at the Adelphi Theatre, New York* ABOVE *Polyna Stoska as Anna and Anne Jeffreys as Rose at the end of* Street Scene *in its original production*

or destroyed), and an overall view of Weill's European career has been impossible to obtain; by the fact that, despite the brilliance of the earlier pieces, the first Brecht scores are also Weill's first fully mature works, and that, as David Drew has pointed out,[1] a certain fashionable nostalgia for the Berlin of the 1920s and 1930s has drawn people towards those Weill-Brecht pieces that seem to reflect what is now regarded as the spirit of that period with the result that the works which do not employ jazz or popular elements (including a number of works with libretti by Brecht) have been ignored. At the same time musical developments in Europe since the Second World War have taken a course to which Weill seems to have little relevance and there have, therefore, been few purely musical studies of Weill's work. The additional consideration that much (though by no means all) of Weill's American music is, without doubt, of a lower standard than his European works has reinforced the popular view that Weill could produce works of any value only when inspired and guided by Brecht.

But perhaps Brecht's own writings, and the writings of the large number of Brecht scholars, have been the most important influences on the formation of the view that sees Weill merely as Brecht's musical factotum. Given the lack of any biographies of Weill until very recently or of any edition of Weill's writings (as compared to the innumerable translations, discussions and commentaries on Brecht); given the fact that we live, at least in Britain and America, in a culture that is literary rather than musical in its orientation, and given, also, Brecht's own flair for self-publicity, it is hardly surprising that Weill's contribution has been regarded as minimal.

Brecht was always cavalier in his treatment of both his sources and his collaborators and it is difficult not to view his biased accounts of the relationship between himself and Weill as being deliberate attempts at enhancing his own stature and achievements. Thus, in an interview published in Copenhagen in March 1934, Brecht suggested that it was because of his understanding of the requirements of a work and his ability to impose his ideas upon others that his musical collaborators gained any success; he once said: 'I had my own composers who knew how to write exactly in my style'.[2] Similarly, in his essay *On the Use of Music in an Epic Theatre*, Brecht implied that it was thanks to him that Weill saw the error of his earlier ways and was thus able to create a new popular style in keeping with the requirements of the drama:

> This type of song was created on the occasion of the Baden-Baden Music Festival of 1927 . . . when I asked Weill to write new settings for half-a-dozen already existing songs. Up to that time Weill had written relatively complicated music of a mainly psychological sort and when he agreed to set to music a series of more or less banal song texts he was making a courageous break with the prejudice which the solid bulk of serious composers held.[3]

Such claims by Brecht have been almost universally accepted as factual descriptions of the relationship between Brecht and Weill. Thus, Otto Friedrich quotes Nicolas Nabakov as saying, 'Brecht was much the stronger of the two. He had to force Weill to write differently'[4] and John Gutmann, the critic of the *Bösen Courier*, as remarking, 'Weill started out as an academic revolutionary. His early works, the Violin Concerto and *The Tzar Has His Picture Taken*, were all atonal. Nobody will ever want to hear them unless he's writing a dissertation on Weill. Brecht wasn't interested in that kind of thing.'[5]

It would, of course, be wrong to suggest that Brecht had little or no impact on Weill. Nonetheless, the view of the relationship between the two men which assumes that Weill not only changed his style to suit Brecht's requirements, but also that he had no view on the theatre and the rôle of music in the theatre other than those which originated in Brecht, shows little understanding of Weill's artistic and intellectual development. In fact, in the years immediately preceding his first collaboration with Brecht, Weill had not only begun to simplify his musical style but had already employed a number of those techniques which were later to be associated with Brecht's epic theatre.

Although the concept of an epic theatre – the essential point of which 'is that it appeals less to the feelings than to the spectator's reason'[6] – appears in Brecht's writings in 1927, the first full exposition of the idea appears in his 1930 article 'Note to the Opera *Aufstieg und Fall der Stadt Mahagonny*'. In this article he criticizes traditional opera and theatre which, he argues, are designed to entertain the spectator by providing him with sensations and encouraging him to become involved in and experience at second hand the events on the stage. Previous attempts at renovating opera have been misguided because they have accepted the apparatus of the form and have thus accepted that the primary function of opera is to provide an evening's entertainment. In place of such 'entertainment' Brecht advocates a new 'epic' theatre and opera in which the listener is forced to view the action as a detached observer, criticizing, judging and making decisions about what is happening on the stage. Emotional involvement, which would interfere with the listener's capacity to make objective judgments, is to be discouraged by means of various alienating devices: the Wagnerian concept of a *Gesamstkunstwerk* – in which music, text, stage direction, costume and all the other elements of a theatrical production work together to produce a total artistic experience – is to be replaced by an opera in which the different elements are clearly separated; the composer is to demonstrate a political and moral attitude rather than express an emotion and the music is to set forth, rather than heighten, the text. Some idea of the ways in which Brecht's theories were to be put into practice can be gained from the descriptions, quoted in earlier chapters, of the first productions of *The Threepenny Opera* and *Der Flug der Lindberghs*.

The '*Mahagonny* Notes' were written after Brecht and Weill had finished the opera, at a time when Brecht's ideas were changing and when the collaboration between the two men was virtually over. Weill was not consulted on the text of the 'Notes' and, in fact, probably disagreed with much that Brecht says in this essay. Nonetheless, many of the alienation techniques which Brecht describes in this article had already been employed – and employed for reasons similar to those put forward by Brecht – in Weill's pre-Brecht works.

For some years before his meeting with Brecht, Weill had been arguing the need for a thoroughgoing re-assessment of the nature and function of opera and for the renewal of operatic form. By 1925-6 Weill had already arrived at many of the ideas which were to characterize his later works. The decisive influence on Weill's conception of opera was his teacher Busoni whose two mature operas, *Arlecchino* (1917) and *Doktor Faust* (1925) stand in direct opposition to the Wagnerian musical and dramatic techniques that dominated German opera in the first decades of the twentieth century. An opera, like a symphony, argued Busoni, should have a musical form that was independent of words or action. It should deal only with those subjects that were incomplete without music and should not attempt to portray what could already be seen on the stage itself. To attempt to describe something in music was to assign to the art a task which lay outside its nature.[8] In rejecting the conventions of the Wagnerian music-drama Busoni advocated a return to the moral and ritualistic attitude of works such as Mozart's *The Magic Flute* and demanded:

> a casting off of what is 'sensuous' and the renunciation of subjectivity (in favour of an objectivity which comes from the author standing back from his work – a purifying road, a hard road, a trial by fire and water) and the reconquest of serenity. Neither Beethoven's wry smile nor Zarathustra's 'liberating laugh' but the smile of wisdom, of divinity and of absolute music. Not profundity, and personal feelings and metaphysics but music which is absolute, distilled and never under a mask of figures and ideas which are borrowed from other spheres.[9]

Edward Dent described the effect of Busoni's 'reforms' in *Doktor Faust* in terms that are immediately reminiscent of those which Brecht employs in his description of the aims of epic theatre. *Doktor Faust*, says Dent, has 'something of the puppet play in its remoteness from everyday sentiments and sentimentality: the figures in the drama do only what is necessary and no more . . . there is no chance for the actors to endear themselves to the audience . . . to appeal to the affection rather than the intellect of the spectator.'[10]

Busoni's views, and his demonstration in the music of *Arlecchino* and of *Doktor Faust* of how these theories could be made to operate in practice, had a deep influence on Weill.

By 1925-6 Weill had already written a number of articles in which he had publicly rejected the dramatic and emotional ethos of late nineteenth-century opera with its would-be psychological profundity:

> for here the experience of the inner soul was so complicated or so superficial that the simplest, the most basic, the oldest and yet the newest emotions were forgotten. It is just these emotions, however, which move us. In this context we can understand why Wagner had to create the form of the music drama, for how could the string quartet, the symphony or the opera suffice when the only function of his art was to mirror the sentiments of larger than life figures, gods, kings and heroes? But we can understand the reasons for his success: for the brutality, the eroticism, the criminality of these works did not express the noblest, but rather the most common human emotions of the pre-war generation.[11]

He stated his belief that the 'music dramas of the past decades' had led opera away from its true goal because they had encouraged 'the abandonment of a purely music framework':

> Musical form is more than just an assemblage of isolated pieces: it is a means of expression every bit as important as the other active components of a composition, and to renounce it, or even to subordinate it, has the effect of significantly curtailing the possible means of musical expression.[12]

The new opera, declared Weill:

> will not be confined to the mere underlining of a dramatic event through expression, tempo, musical pitch and dynamic: it goes far beyond that. It is a unique and purely musical art form, developed in close proximity with the theatre, and cannot be merely the adding of a theatrical expression or Gest to a musical event, nor of illustrating a dramatic plot with music. The interaction of a plot which enhances the music, or of music which only provides a commentary to the events on stage, does not make an opera.[13]

As an example of the way in which music and drama could combine to produce a new form of heightened theatre, a 'reinterpretation of naturalistic effects', Weill cites the 'alienating' effect achieved at the moment in Busoni's *Doktor Faust* 'when Mephistopheles murders the believers at the gate; the music leaves the interpretation of the outrageous event to the imagination of the listener and contents itself with a gesture of gentleness and freedom.'[14]

It is in his 1926 article on Busoni's *Doktor Faust* that Weill uses, for the first time, the word 'Gest', a term that occupies an important position in the development of Brecht's ideas on epic theatre but does not appear in Brecht's own writings until the '*Mahagonny* Notes' which were written in 1930. The term denotes 'an attitude, or a single aspect of an attitude, expressible in words or actions'. In 1929 Weill published an essay *'On the Gestic Character of Music'* and, in the same year, published another article in which he developed the ideas he had first stated in his Busoni article of 1926:

> The new theatrical form, in which the chorus again plays an important role, creates a wholly new set of conditions for the use of music in the theatre, for this type of theatre is mainly concerned with the outward going 'gestures' of the production and, therefore, it leaves a great deal of scope for the musical score – not to illustrate or advance the plot,

> but to grasp and underline the basic ideogrammatic attitudes expressed in a series of separate scenes . . . it is no longer enough merely to add a few images and the prerequisites of modern living to the existing form of music drama; nor is it enough to adopt a frivolous attitude to the problems of form in the use of music theatre. The subject matter of the time must find its equivalent in the form of contemporary music theatre.[15]

By the time the above essay had been written, Weill and Brecht had been collaborating for over three years (indeed, the collaboration was almost over) and each had, undoubtedly, influenced the other's views. Nonetheless, the ideas expressed in this article are not only those expressed in the articles written in 1925-6 but those which Weill demonstrated in a number of compositions written before he began working with Brecht.

The Protagonist, Weill's first theatrical success, was the first practical demonstration of the kind of 'new operatic form' which he had advocated in his writings. The story of the opera concerns the leader of a troupe of actors in Shakespearean England – the Protagonist himself – whose sense of identification with his fictitious theatrical rôles becomes so great that it invades, and eventually destroys, his sense of reality. The work is thus directly concerned with one of the basic ideas underlying Brecht's theories of epic theatre – the extent to which emotional involvement in an art can obscure both a sense of reality and an ability to make moral judgments. In order to emphasize the subject of the opera, and to prevent the kind of emotional involvement which the work itself condemns, Weill deliberately distances the listener from the drama by writing music which is quite distinct from the stage action which it accompanies. Perhaps the clearest and most startling example of Weill's techniques comes at the very end of the opera when art and reality have finally become one to the Protagonist and, having murdered his own sister, he pleads to be allowed to give one last, great performance in which there will no longer be 'any distinction between real and feigned madness'. Avoiding the traditional 'distracted' mad scene, in which the music would merely illustrate the mental state of the Protagonist, Weill chooses to accompany the stage action at this point with music of the most simple, triadic kind – the little fanfares for the on-stage wind band shown in Ex 3. Coming after the complex chromaticism of the earlier music, this triadic music has a clarity and a triviality which forms a fitting comment on the banality and emptiness of the Protagonist's own artistic beliefs; by going against, rather than simply illustrating, the stage action the music demonstrates a moral attitude towards the dramatic events.[16]

Ex 3 The Protagonist

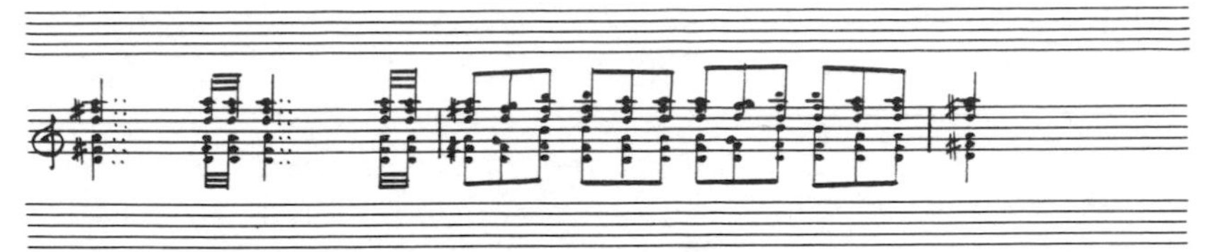

The similarity between the techniques which Weill employs in this, his first performed opera and those which Brecht was to advocate in his 1930 '*Mahagonny* Notes' hardly needs pointing out. *The Protagonist* already demonstrates many of the elements of Brecht's epic theatre and all the leading critics of the time were quick to observe the effectiveness and the novelty of Weill's approach. Writing about the première of the work for the Berlin *Bösen Courier*, Oskar Bie remarked on the anti-romantic aspects of the piece: 'The romantic aching is over, scenic and spiritual shadows are brightly lit and the expression of feeling in the music is somehow hardened'[17] while Maurice Abravanel observed that Weill:

> full of enthusiasm and inspired by the objectivity of the Russians, has composed an opera that is without concession and without triviality . . . Weill does not weep at the death of the sister and nowhere does he invite us to take part in the despair of the hero – he satisfies himself with showing it, but does so with an accuracy that thrills the listener. This gives the work its peculiar value. *The Protagonist* is, as far as I know, the first successful attempt in opera to move the audience without engaging its sympathy.[18]

Adorno spoke of the fact that the music 'in no way mirrored the drama' but worked through disassociation, and was the key to the 'deep-lying dramatic intentions'[19] of the piece. All the critics recognized the work as being what Heinrich Strobel described as 'the beginning of a new development which clearly and resolutely leads to a new type of opera'.[20]

While developing his ideas on the relations between music and text in the 'new opera' Weill was also beginning to re-examine the nature of his musical language. Writing about *The Protagonist* in 1926 he said that his work on the opera had shown him not only that the 'stage had its own musical form which grows out of the course of the stage action' but also that 'on the stage, meaningful things can only be said with the simplest, most inconspicuous of means.'[21]

The triadic music at the end of *The Protagonist* had been a theatrical 'effect', a musical comment depending for its force on the complex, chromatic nature of the music which preceded it. In the works which followed *The Protagonist* – *Royal Palace*, *The New Orpheus* and *The Tsar Has His Photograph Taken* – Weill began deliberately to simplify his musical style and to create a new language in which triadic formations became the norm, in which the rhythmic figurations and the phrase structures became more immediately comprehensible, in which the frequent changes of bar length disappear and in which the accompanimental figures acquire a distinctly 'popular' feel. Already in these works the music is within striking distance, if not of the more overtly jazz-based *Threepenny Opera* and *Happy End*, then at least of that mixture of wiry neo-classicism and popular music which characterizes *Mahagonny*. As the following two examples demonstrate, the ostinato patterns and the melodic figurations of these works are often strikingly similar to those of the later *Mahagonny:*

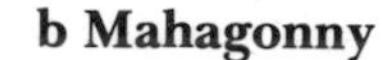

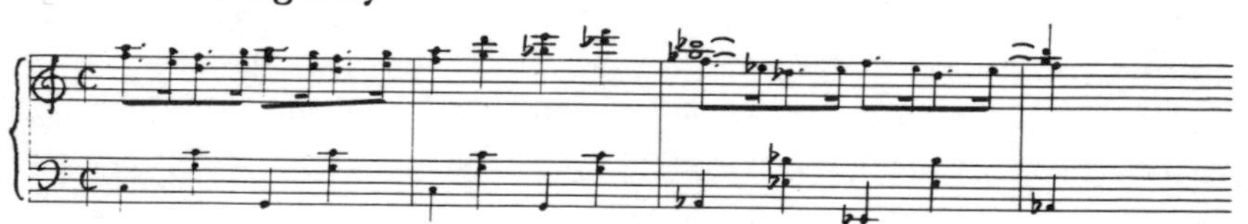

Ex 5, also from *Der Zar*, shows an early example of the kind of peculiarly Weillian side-step that is so typical of his later music:

Ex 5

Particularly interesting are such passages as that, from *Der Zar*, shown in Ex 6 below:

Ex 6

In this passage the highly chromatic melodic line, with its angular and unpredictable contour, seems to look back to the Schoenbergian expressionism of the early instrumental works while the other elements of the music – the rhythmic patterns, the neatly balancing, four-square phrase structures and the vamp-like accompaniment figuration – are clearly derived from the kind of popular model that Weill was to employ in his later pieces. Such passages are audible demonstrations of the link between his early and mature styles: once one has heard such a passage it is not difficult to understand how the sudden harmonic shifts and the unexpected melodic turns which characterize Weill's later work came about as a result of the bringing together of such apparently opposed influences as popular music, Viennese expressionism and Busonian neo-classicism. *Der Zar* and the two Goll works also mark the first appearance of jazz and popular elements in Weill's music. However, in all three works popular music is employed as a 'special effect', for specific dramatic purposes. In *Royal Palace* the jazz-influenced numbers accompany a film scene which depicts the heroine's pursuit of various fashionable pleasures – a train journey to Constantinople, a visit to Nice, to a ball, to the Russian Ballet, by aeroplane to the North Pole. In *Der Zar* the jazz number is a tango which, played on a gramophone, accompanies the Tsar's attempts to seduce the young lady photographer who, unknown to him, has come to assassinate him. Although satirical in effect, the function of these jazz numbers is, therefore, comparable to that of the triadic music which ends *The Protagonist*. The popular elements are employed as 'quotations', references to a musical style outside that of the main body of the piece, which thus make their effect through their incongruity. Like the triadic music of *The Protagonist* the jazz numbers of these pre-Brecht works express a moral attitude to the events happening on the stage. They condemn the frivolous and empty life of the heroine of *Royal Palace* and comment on the Tsar's sensuality and gullibility in *Der Zar*.

It is unfortunate that the music of the opera *Na und . . .* has almost completely disappeared since this piece might well have proved to be the key work in an attempt to understand Weill's development during this period. According to David Drew, the few remaining sketches for *Na und . . .* show that Weill later used many of the musical ideas from the piece in *Mahagonny*.[22] As it is, *The Mahagonny Songspiel*, *The Threepenny Opera* and, above all, the *Mahagonny* opera stand as the first works in which popular elements are fully assimilated into Weill's music and become the basis of a new and more easily comprehensible style. In these works the popular elements are no longer employed, as they are in the earlier operas, as deliberately incongruous, and thus satirical, features. The moral attitude expressed by the jazz music of *Royal Palace* and *Der Zar* is, however, implicit in Weill's use of popular music in the later works.

The nature and purpose of the simpler and more popular style towards which Weill was moving during the mid-1920s, and which he first fully adopted in the Brecht works, has been frequently misunderstood. Jazz and popular elements form only a small part of this new style. However, since general interest in Weill's music has been, almost exclusively, confined to those works which exploit popular music elements, it is a part that has attracted considerable attention.

Weill was not alone among serious composers in expressing an interest in jazz. For a while many composers – including men of the stature of Ravel, Debussy and Stravinsky, as well as lesser composers such as Krenek, Milhaud and the other members of Les Six – experimented with the possibility of employing some aspect of jazz in their music. Even the members of the Second Viennese School were affected by this trend. Both Schoenberg and Webern employed jazz instruments in at least one work each, although Berg was the only one of the three Viennese composers to use anything resembling the actual rhythms and figurations of jazz in his music. In some cases, such as that of Stravinsky, an interest in jazz seems to have been occasioned by a purely intellectual interest in its rhythmic techniques. In other cases the interest may have come about because, since the decline of tonality inevitably raised questions about the rhythmic, as well as the pitch, organization of music, dance rhythms of all kinds seemed to offer a way of generating some sense of momentum; in such cases an interest in jazz was comparable to the neo-classical composers' interest in baroque dance forms.

Weill's interest in jazz and popular music falls into neither of these categories. Nor can his jazz-influenced works be regarded simply as one manifestation of the idea, popular in the Germany of his period, of 'Zeitoper' or 'opera of the time' – of opera which, using jazz and the other fashionable music of the day, dealt with modern people in realistic, modern settings doing modern, up-to-date things. Krenek's 1927 'jazz opera' *Jonny spielt auf* is perhaps the best known example of Zeitoper. Although Weill is often regarded as one of the leading representatives of the Zeitoper composers, he himself resented the term, believing it suggested that topicality and 'relevance' in the arts meant nothing more than fashionable sensationalism. He regarded the idea of Zeitoper as an excuse for avoiding a thorough re-examination of operatic form.

Attacking the naive idea that there was a simple correlation between theatrical 'relevance' and mere fashion, Weill argued, in an essay on *Aktuelles Theater* (written in 1929), that the influence of the events of the time was clearly recognizable in the dramas of all periods and that the great spiritual and political movements of the day had always been handled by the theatre. Though based on historic truths, works such as Mozart's *The Marriage of Figaro* and Beethoven's *Fidelio* expressed a moral and spiritual truth, and thus had an enduring topicality, that placed them far above the genre of 'Zeitstücke' or period pieces. In an article on *Mahagonny*, Weill specifically rejects the idea that the catchwords 'Zeitoper', 'Jazz opera' and so on, as they have become understood are applicable to the work. 'Zeitoper', 'Zeittheater', 'Aktualität' and all such terms, argued Weill, had become catchwords, presented as though they represented the main problems of the theatre of the day:

> In this the situation in the theatre generally accords with the political situation in Germany, in that a concept that could have had a positive value and produced some kind of movement forward has, through the levelling effects of coalition politics, become a reactionary danger . . . These cheap forms of 'actuality' have been seized on by the conservative theatre; they alter nothing of the traditional forms; they don't change the way in which one really perceives anything and their effect on the box office is minimal . . . everything that we have experienced in the last year of 'the rhythm of the machine', the 'tempo of the city', the 'melody of the skyscrapers' and such like belong to these cheap forms.[23]

Weill published two articles on jazz. The first, entitled *Dancemusic: Jazz* was written in March 1926, two months after he had completed *Royal Palace*, the work in which the influence of jazz is first clearly observable. This article thus predates Weill's meeting with Brecht by precisely one year and the composition of the *Mahagonny Songspiel* by some fourteen months. In the article Weill draws attention to both the social significance of popular music and to the distinction between jazz and dance music:

> Today, because it is one of the few activities which can make city dwellers forget their humdrum everyday lives, dance has a significance that it did not possess in earlier times. It has, on the one hand, led to the growth of a light music industry which has little to do with art; on the other hand, however, some parts of dance music so completely define the spirit of the age that they could exert a lasting influence over a specific part of serious 'art music'.
>
> The rhythm of our time is jazz. In it the slow but sure

> Americanisation of all our physical life finds its most notable manifestation.
>
> Unlike art music, dance music reproduces nothing of the perceptions of the exceptional individual who stands above his times; instead it mirrors the instinct of the masses. And a glance into any of the dance halls of any continent shows that jazz is as precise the external expression of our time as was the waltz of the nineteenth century.
>
> Even the inveterate opponent of this 'spirit of the time' will admit that, in those places which give forth dance music all evening, the shimmy outweighs everything else.
>
> But if one plays a syncopated 2/2 bar underneath, it still doesn't make it jazz. The negro music, from which the jazz band originally sprang, is full of a rhythm complexity, of deft harmonic traits, of timbral and modulatory niceties of a kind that most of our dance band leaders are simply incapable . . . We have, for some weeks now, had a chance to hear real jazz bands on the radio for whole evenings . . . everything else that the radio offers us as dance music is surrogate.[24]

In his *Article on Jazz*, written in 1929 when he had already composed many of those jazz-based pieces on which his popular fame rests, Weill observed:

> Jazz appears, within a time when artistry is increasing, as a piece of nature, as the most healthy and powerful expression of an art which, because of its popular origins, has immediately become an international folk music of the broadest possible consequences. Why should art-music isolate itself from such an influence? It depended on the strength of those individual talents who were approached by jazz, whether or not they could maintain their position under this influence; and for the serious European musician it was out of the question to imitate American dance music, let alone ennoble it.[25]

The distinction which Weill draws, in the first of these articles, between popular dance music and pure jazz is an important one. Weill's music has little relation to true jazz. The jazz influences that appear in his music are those which appeared in the popular dance music of the time; the tempo directions and the markings that stand at the head of each number in *The Threepenny Opera*, and which are not in the usual Italian, all relate to popular dance forms of the period, such as the foxtrot, the shimmy, the Boston and the tango.

To Weill, the main attraction of such popular music was that it produced an 'international folk music of the broadest consequences'; it provided him with a musical style which reflected 'the instinct of the masses', upon which he could build an individual and easily comprehensible style capable of dealing with the 'great ideas of the age'.

As a member of the Novembergrüppe, Weill subscribed to the group's belief in the social function of art. His social, political and artistic beliefs thus demanded that he write music that was comprehensible to a large body of people, and not simply to a small élite. An awareness of the social obligations of the artist informs all Weill's music from 1925 onwards and also runs through his writings. From the outset his articles as Berlin correspondent of *Der Deutsche Rundfunk* concentrate on the social responsibilities of the radio as an instrument which is directly in touch with a large section of the population.

Writing, in 1929, about *The Berlin Requiem*, Weill described the emergence of his new style as being determined by both social and technical considerations:

> The cantata *The Berlin Requiem* is one of a number of works that were, to a certain extent, thought of as studies for the opera *The Rise and Fall of the City of Mahagonny*.
>
> These works employ a certain type of vocal style with a small orchestra which is handled in such a way that the piece can be presented in the concert hall, in the form of a cantata, but can equally well – because of the attempt to make the musical speech clear and because of the way in which the gestic aspects of the content are determined – be presented in the theatre. It cannot be difficult to develop such a form, which meets equally the demands of the theatre and the concert hall, to meet the requirements of the radio. The bases of a radio art are: a strong musical structuring which suits the spiritual content of the work and which has the potential for a scenic production, but is compelling enough musically to enable the listener, without the help of the stage, to see in his mind a picture of the people who speak to him. It is thus handled here not as a lyric and not as the description of a condition but as the representation of a model. Having to write these pieces of

> music for radio obviously meant that I had to know about the acoustic restrictions of the broadcasting studio; about which instrumental and orchestral possibilities the microphone favoured; about the spread of vocal registers and the harmonic limitations which radio imposes. Several years' observation of listeners to radio music and some experiments of my own, have shown me that it is the clarity and the transparency, rather than the refinement of the instrumental sound that is important. The radio presents serious musicians today, for the first time, with the problem of writing works which can be assimilated by a large group of listeners. The contents and the form of these radio compositions must, therefore, capture the interest of a large number of people of all sorts while the means of musical expression must present no difficulties to the inexperienced listener. Without doubt, the contents of *The Berlin Requiem* mirror the feelings and fears of a large majority of people. It is an attempt to express what the city-dweller of our time has to say about the idea of death.[26]

The simplification of Weill's musical style in the mid 1920s (a simplification which, as we have seen, began some time before his meeting with Brecht) was not therefore simply the result of the different musical demands of the theatre as opposed to the concert hall. It was also a response to what Weill, in common with his fellow members of the Novembergrüppe and many other artists in the Weimar Republic, regarded as the social demands of the time. Art had a social function which could not be met by writing for an élite, but only by developing a language which would be generally comprehensible. Weill is reported to have said 'I am not struggling for new forms or new theories, I am struggling for a new public.'[27]

Weill's purpose in employing jazz and popular elements was not, therefore – as is often suggested – parodistic. It was not his intention to mock either those popular forms which he used as his models or the conventions of traditional opera. Weill clarified his attitude to parody in an interview he gave in April 1930 on *Der Jasager*. When Dr Hans Fischer, the interviewer, remarked that it was those 'parodistic elements' of Weill's music, which were lacking in *Der Jasager*, that had made his earlier works so successful with young people, Weill replied:

> Perhaps we should talk of a serious-ironical style, for the irony in *The Threepenny Opera* is meant seriously. People are

> mistaken if they have understood *The Threepenny Opera* only as a parody, as 'a lark'. Modern composers are not, in general, parodistically inclined – as the public and critics seem to believe. We are serious in subject and in music.[28]

Direct parodies of popular music appear in Weill's music only when dramatically justified. Thus, the banality of the refrain which accompanies the various self-indulgences in Act II of *Mahagonny* is itself a deliberate comment on the futility of the lives led by the characters involved. Similarly the cheap emotionalism of the dreadful 'Maiden's Prayer' in Act I of the same work (a number which elicits an enraptured 'That is eternal art' from one listener) is a reflection of the emotional shallowness of those characters. Parodies of the conventions of traditional opera are almost completely absent, as one might expect given not only Weill's love of Mozart and other eighteenth- and nineteenth-century operas but also his views on the seriousness of the form. Perhaps the only overt parody of operatic convention in Weill's work is the 'Jealousy Duet' between Lucy and Polly in Act II of *The Threepenny Opera*, a number which is as much an affectionate reference to operatic conventions as is Mozart's parody of the excesses of *opera seria* in Fiordiligi's distraught aria in Act I of *Così Fan Tutte*.

In describing Weill's work as 'music with a smouldering vividness and, at the same time, a mortally sad and faded background, music with a circumspect sharpness which, by means of its leaps and side-steps, makes articulate something that the song public would prefer not to know about,'[29] Adorno has pointed to the real relationship between Weill's music and that of the popular music of the time. Frederic Ewen has remarked that 'Post-war Germany had constructed out of America a fabulous, visionary domain, partly concocted out of reality, mostly built out of fantasy.'[30] The American dollar was 'seen as a sort of radiant vision against the background of the nightmare collapse of the mark', and there was:

> the American dream of Walt Whitman, the American West of the Indians, the grand adventure of the open prairies, buffaloes, cowboys and, not least, the lure of the great American cities with their skyscrapers. Everything that was American – American dances, Negro jazz, American drinks, American gangsters, American boxers, American speech – enjoyed a fashionable vogue.[31]

In taking these popular American forms as his models Weill relates not to the dance hall and the Amusierenkabaret, where such forms were most popular, but to the true literary tradition of the German cabaret. Cabaret style and techniques were, of course, an important influence on both Weill and Brecht. Brecht had himself set up a cabaret, *Die Rote Zibebe*, in Munich in 1922 and had made his first appearance in Berlin singing in cabaret to the accompaniment of his own guitar. One of Brecht's earliest writings is a description of a cabaret performance by Frank Wedekind: 'A few weeks ago he sang with his guitar, with a brittle voice, monotonous and untrained. Never has a singer so moved and inspired me.'[32]

The extent to which Brecht modelled his own cabaret style on that of Wedekind can be judged by comparing the above description with Lion Feuchtwanger's description of Brecht's own cabaret performances:

> He planted himself in the middle of the room and with open effrontery, in a horrible, loud shrill voice began to deliver his ballads to the twanging of a banjo, pronouncing his words with an unmistakably broad accent.[33]

Brecht's use of the word 'song' in the title of the *Mahagonny Songspiel* is a deliberate attempt to indicate that the pieces are cabaret rather than art songs. Both *The Threepenny Opera* and *Happy End* were written for, and originally performed by, cabaret singers and actors rather than trained singers. But the cabaret influence in these works is much deeper than its effects on performance techniques. Weill's use of his popular music models is directly comparable to the way in which Wedekind, Tucholsky, Mehring and the other great cabaret writers employed popular and immediately recognizable literary forms as the vehicle for the most searching examination of the political and social ills of the period.

Weill regarded his use of the popular forms and idioms of the time as being an essentially traditional technique that was in no way different from Bach's use of baroque dance forms, Beethoven's use of the minuet or Brahms' of the waltz. In many ways Weill's appropriation of popular idioms can be seen, not as part of a general interest in jazz, but as an extension of the neo-classicism which he inherited from Busoni. The way in which Weill employs his popular models is remarkably similar to the way in which the neo-classical composers of the period employed their chosen baroque or classical models.

In his essay on *The Threepenny Opera*, Adorno analyzed Weill's techniques by comparing the 'foreground' – the music Weill actually wrote – to the implied popular background in which 'the fatuous diminished seventh chords, the chromatic alteration of diatonic melodic steps, the espressivo that expresses nothing, all sound false to us.' So, Adorno says:

> Weill makes the chords themselves false by adding to the triad another note which sounds as false as did a true triad in the dance music of the 1890s, he distorts the melodic steps, he shows the stupidity of the modulation which doesn't go anywhere or shifts the modulatory emphasis in such a way as to upset the harmonic proportions so that a compositional style which includes a modulation from nothing to nothing itself collapses into an abyss of nothingness. There is a very clear path from such techniques to the best radical Stravinsky, such as *The Soldier's Tale* or the piano duets.[34]

Adorno's remarks suggest that he regarded Weill's intentions as being essentially parodistic (it is significant that he chooses as a comparison the little piano duets which are amongst the most overtly parodistic of Stravinsky's works). Nevertheless, his perception of the similarity between Weill and Stravinsky, and of the relation between foreground event and background model in the music of each composer, is quite accurate. Although working against very different background models, both Weill and Stravinsky employ these models in a similar way and both are careful to select only those aspects of the original models that will further their own creative ends. With both composers the result is a series of pieces in which the chosen 'model' acts as an ever-present and recognizable background against which the music operates; the works make their effect through the listener's perception of the difference between the 'heard' foreground and the 'understood' background. Moreover, in both Weill and Stravinsky the effect of this technique is to produce an emotional objectivity, a 'distancing' or – to use a term that has become particularly associated with Brecht – a sense of alienation which encourages the listener to consider and think about, rather than become emotionally involved in the music. The sense of objectivity which these techniques produce is, in itself, an indication of the extent to which Weill's music accords with the spirit of neo-classicism and of much of the art of the period.

Neo-classicism in music was a positive rejection of the hyperemotional romanticism of much post-Wagnerian composition; a rejection of expressionism in music, akin to that rejection of expressionism in the literary and visual arts which took place after the First War. In France, in *Le Coq et L'Arlequin*, Cocteau called for 'an end to music in which one lies and soaks', to music 'which has to be listened to with one's face in one's hands', and demanded 'Musical bread', 'music I can live in like a house',[35] suggesting the music hall, the circus and American negro bands as things which might fertilize an artist's imagination. Cocteau's pamphlet inspired much of the music of Les Six and set the tone of French music in the 1920s. In France the anti-romanticism of Les Six and their colleagues often resulted in facile and self-indulgent triviality; Weill's aims were more serious and purposeful.

Ian Kemp, in what, as yet, remains the only serious study of Weill's techniques, has defined a number of the elements which contribute to the ambiguous and peculiarly Weillian emotional climate of the works of the 1920s and 1930s. On the harmonic level Professor Kemp observes that 'whereas such figures as Stravinsky, Hindemith, Prokofiev and Milhaud tended (in returning to tonality) to reject traditional harmonic usage, Weill proceeded to develop a largely triadic harmony, paring down his vocabulary to the most basic chords and progressions.'[36] Professor Kemp has elsewhere observed that:

> the harmonic novelty in Weill's works lies in the way in which simple harmonies are juxtaposed; such juxtapositions creating a 'directional ambiguity', a sense of inner dissonance more disturbing than the overt dissonances of many works which may sound much harsher . . . from the consequent tension between the sophistication of the harmony and the simplicity of the phrasing arises a part of that strange ambiguity which pervades the entire structure and feeling of Weill's music . . . its compelling strength owes much to a tension between the familiar . . . and the striking novelty of the harmonic palette.[37]

Two examples from *Mahagonny* will serve to illustrate the extent to which the kind of tensions described by Professor Kemp operate at all levels of Weill's music.

The 'Alabama Song' consists of two contrasted halves. The opening of the first is shown in Ex 7a; and of the second in Ex 7b.

Moderato assai
Jenny
p
Oh show us the way to the
next whis-ky bar
6 Girls
Oh don't ask why
For we must find the next
Oh don't ask why
X
Y
Z
whis-ky bar, for if we don't find the next whis-ky

Ex 7 b

Melodically the first half employs only the very simplest and most confined of patterns – three notes, descending in step, which together cover the interval of a minor third; the minor third C – A in the phrases for solo voice, mirrored by the minor third A – F sharp in the alternating chorus phrases. Only at the very end of the first half of the song, as the music moves towards the cadence which introduces the 'refrain' of the second half, does the melodic line momentarily break out of these narrow limits. The simplicity of this melodic pattern, and its initial presentation as two regularly balancing, symmetrical phrases (the four-bar phrase, marked 'x' in Ex 7a, on the solo voice, answered by the complementary four-bar phrase 'y' for the chorus of six girls) acts as a fixed and easily recognizable norm against which the less predictable elements operate.

Through its very obsessiveness the constant repetition of this simple, rather matter-of-fact, opening pattern creates a certain tension. A further tension is introduced into the repetition of the opening melodic line, at bar ten, when the regularity of the previously symmetrical phrase structures is broken by the unexpected extension of the second solo phrase to create an asymmetrical seven-bar phrase ('z' in Ex 7a). At the same time the descending three-note pattern C, B, A shifts its position in the bar, thus disturbing the established relationship between the melodic figuration and the downbeat or rhythmically strong first beat of the bar.

This opening melodic line is supported by an orchestral accompaniment which, in terms of key, is highly ambiguous and constantly refuses to confirm or deny a stable tonality. Considered in isolation the vocal melody of this first half seems to imply a clear A minor tonality, the solo phrases being centred around the tonic A and the chorus phrases around the dominant E. However, such an interpretation is undermined at the outset by the fact that the opening figure in the accompaniment suggests C minor – a suggestion that is never confirmed since the harmonies throughout the first section are ambiguous, while the chief harmonic and tonal event of the opening twenty-four bars is the side-step in the bass from the opening C – G pedal to a pedal on C sharp and F sharp (a side-step between two extremely remote tonal areas which are separated by the interval of a tritone).

Ambiguous in its direction and unstable in its tonality, the opening half of the song acts as a long upbeat into the 'refrain' of the second half when the tonal uncertainties are finally resolved and the piece settles into a clear G major. In contrast to the confined melodic line of the first half, the vocal line (now completely symmetrical in its construction) becomes much more lyrical and wide-ranging in the second half, frequently covering an octave (and sometimes more) within the space of a few bars. The vocal lyricism of this second half takes place, however, against a flat, emotionally neutral accompaniment consisting of simple chords (enlivened only by some internal chromaticism and, when repeated, a few fragmentary melodic figurations) stated as a mechanically-repeated rhythmic figuration. The vocal line moves in long four-bar phrases in which one feels the move towards the strong downbeats at the beginning of the first and third bars; the accompanying figure is much more terse, covering only half a bar and appearing on the downbeat. The simultaneous use of a romantically lyrical vocal line and an accompanying figure which studiously avoids the upbeat – with its feeling of leaning towards the next bar and its traditionally expressive connotations – is a typically Weillian ambiguity. Together the melody and the accompaniment undermine, and consequently neutralize, one another. The emotional ambiguity and the sense of ironic objectivity produced by this fusion of romantic and anti-romantic gesture lies at the heart of the peculiar fascination exerted by Weill's music of the 1920s and 1930s.

It is interesting to compare the 'Alabama Song', one of the first numbers in the opera, with the 'Benares Song', the 'companion piece' which occupies a similar position at the end of the work. Here again a sixteen-bar introduction (more tonally stable than that of the 'Alabama Song' but similarly marked by surprising side-steps to remote areas) leads – via a peculiarly disorientating *a capella* chord sequence – to a lyrical refrain. Both sections of the song are accompanied by the same repeated rhythmic pattern.

The relationship between the lyrical melodic line and the terse, mechanically repeated accompaniment figure is similar to that found in the refrain of the 'Alabama Song' and produces a similarly 'distancing' effect. In the slow tempo of the 'Benares Song', however, the brashness of the 'Alabama Song' gives way to a sense of tragedy and disillusionment.

The refrain of the 'Benares Song' is shown in Ex 8. Here, in contrast to the 'Alabama Song', the movement towards the downbeat is emphasized both by the placing of the accompaniment's rhythmic figuration and by the yearning suspensions in the upper two vocal lines. The lyricism of these two vocal lines is further emphasized by their moving together in sensuous parallel thirds, by the ecstatic upward leap of a seventh (at 'a' in Ex 8) and by the subsequent descent to the double suspension on to the tonic F major which follows this leap.

Ex 8

Jen.
Let's go, let's go to Be-na-
Begb.
Let's go, let's go to Be-na-
F.
Oh,
Tob.
Oh,
Bill
Oh,
Let us go. let us go, let us go to Be-
M.
no
Let us go, let us go, let us go to Be-
Jen.
-res, to Be-na-res, where the sun is shi--ning. Let's
Begb.
-res, to Be-na-res, where the sun is shi--ning. Let's
F.
let us go let us go to Be-na-res let us go
Tob.
let us go let us go to Be-na-res let us go
Bill
na-res
M.
na-res

Having temporarily achieved this clear F major the harmony then clouds over as it moves back towards the minor key at the final cadence. Here, in the sweetness of the parallel thirds and the luxuriance of the suspensions, Weill subtly employs and exploits the traditional conventions and the emotional associations which these conventions carry. The contrast between the yearning vocal line and the flat, objective rhythmic figuration which accompanies it reveals that the Benares 'where the sun is shining' is nothing more than a romantic and unobtainable dream. By this point in the opera Jimmy, the leading male character, has been sentenced to death and it is clear that the city of Mahagonny can no longer survive. If *Mahagonny* is a criticism of the emptiness of everything that the mythical America represented to the German imagination of the period, then the 'Benares Song' is the number in which the final disillusionment with this myth is most clearly stated. The music itself reveals the emptiness of the illusion. After the move back from the momentary warmth of the F major at the centre of the refrain to the darkness of the F minor cadence, we hardly need to hear that 'Benares is said to have perished in an earthquake' to know that the dream of an escape from the harshness of reality to some imagined paradise has been destroyed forever.

The two songs discussed above demonstrate two of Weill's most characteristic technical procedures: the underpinning of a romantically expressive melodic line by an unemotional, anti-romantic, accompaniment figure and the use of straightforward, regularly balanced phrase structures and simple diatonic melodies in conjunction with ambiguous harmonic formations. These formations tend to side-slip unexpectedly into remote tonal areas, especially those that are a semitone or a tritone away from the previous key centre. In his review of *The Protagonist* Abravanel perceptively points to the influence of the Russian composers on Weill's view of the relationship between text and music in the opera. There is little mention of the Russian composers in Weill's writings, and no mention of Mussorgsky, but the influence of Mussorgsky's modal harmonic procedures is evident in much of Weill's music and, like Mussorgsky, Weill tends to prefer relationships that lie outside the traditional diatonic system of Western music. In places the influence of Mussorgsky invades Weill's melodic, as well as harmonic, patterns; the recurring motif of *The Seven Deadly Sins*, which is discussed below, is instantly reminiscent of sections of Mussorgsky's *Boris Godunov*, while the melody which opens the first movement of *The Berlin Requiem* (shown in Ex 9 below) seems to be a direct quotation of part of Varlaam's song in Act II, Scene 1 of *Boris* (Ex 10).

Ex 9 Berlin Requiem No 1 Grosser Dank Chorale

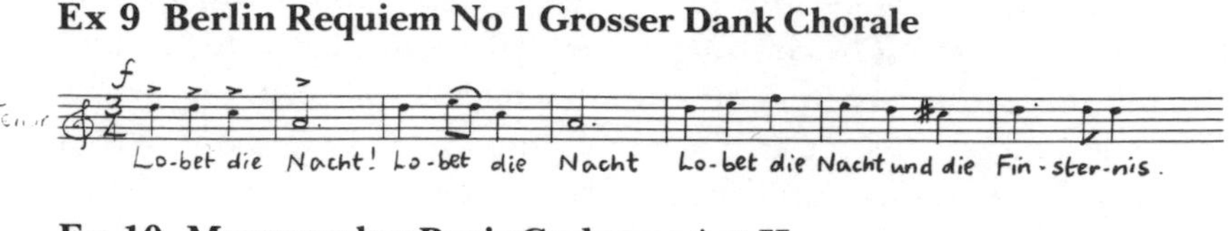

Ex 10 Mussorgsky: Boris Godunov Act II

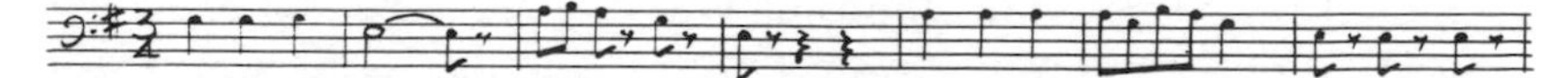

Mussorgsky, the most original and individual of the Russian Nationalist composers, had, of course, been dead for almost forty-five years when Weill wrote *The Protagonist* but his music was, nonetheless, almost unknown in Germany. The French composers of the late-nineteenth and early-twentieth century, and especially Debussy, felt a particular affinity for Russian music. At a time when Debussy was, quite consciously, trying to free himself from the influence of Wagner and the Central European tradition which dominated Western European music, the work of the Russians in general, and of Mussorgsky in particular, seemed to offer a possible alternative. Debussy's harmonic innovations – his use of remote tonal relationships, of parallel triads, of unresolved discords and of the chord as a sonorous object in its own right – were deeply indebted to Mussorgsky's example.

However, although German film and theatre of the Weimar Republic were affected by the examples of the Russians, German composers (deeply conscious of belonging to the great Austro-German musical tradition) remained almost entirely unaffected by Russian influences. Of the German composers of his time, only Weill seems to have understood and absorbed the significance of the music of Mussorgsky and the Russian Nationalists; as in Debussy, it is in Weill's individual handling of harmonic and tonal relationships that this influence reveals itself.

Weill's instrumentation plays a particularly important rôle in achieving the kind of emotional ambiguity discussed above. Adorno referred to *Mahagonny* as 'music with a sonority that is filtered by a handful of instruments and that possesses a power of expansion that routs and leaves behind the diffuseness of a much larger orchestra.'[38] I have already referred to Weill's interest in Mahler and to the possible influence that the chamber-music-like orchestration and the bringing together of clearly contrasted 'unblended' timbres, which one finds in late Mahler, might have had on Weill's orchestral techniques.

To some extent, Weill's use of a small instrumental ensemble in the works of the late 1920s and the 1930s is, of course, an imitation of the sonority of the dance and cabaret bands of the time. However, it is also a reflection of that trend away from the large orchestras of the late-nineteenth century and the early-twentieth century that was general among the composers of the period. To some extent this trend was forced upon composers by purely economic considerations; given the difficult financial situation in Europe after the First World War, a new work for a small instrumental group had more chance of being performed than had a new work which required large orchestral forces. At a deeper level, the reaction against the sumptuous and luxuriant sonorities of the late-romantic orchestra was yet another aspect of the general anti-romantic movement in the arts of the period. Weill's liking for wind and brass timbres is a characteristic manifestation of this anti-romantic trend. Like Stravinsky – and for the same reasons – Weill tends to avoid the string instruments, with their 'expressive', 'romantic' connotations, preferring the more objective, more clearly articulated, non-vibrato sound of the wind instruments. Of the works written in collaboration with Brecht, the scores of *Happy End*, *The Berlin Requiem* and *Der Jasager* include none of the usual orchestral strings; *The Threepenny Opera* and *The Lindbergh Flight* employ only a single cello. Even in those works, such as the *Mahagonny* opera and *The Seven Deadly Sins*, that use a full complement, strings are employed as rhythmic and percussive, rather than cantabile instruments. They are used 'in quotation marks' for consciously romantic effects or are used in such a way that their expressive timbre is neutralized by the simultaneous use of more acerbic timbres. Such a use of the string instruments itself gives rise to that emotional ambiguity, that tension between the romantic and anti-romantic gesture, that is so characteristic of Weill's music.

In the following short passage from *The Seven Deadly Sins*, for example, the almost Mahlerian yearning of the string line is negated by the terse, jazz-like figurations of the wind and muted brass which accompany it:

Ex 11

The clear, sparse textures of the Weill-Brecht works, the lack of any 'filling-in' parts and the sharp, unmixed timbres act as part of the distancing process. There is no indulgence in rich sonorities 'for their own sake': no 'wash of sound' which the listener can allow to flood over him. Any large-scale, rhetorical gesture is immediately reduced in size, and called into question, any romantically expressive figuration immediately endistanced and objectified by being played on such a small group of cleanly articulated, non-expressive instruments.

The popular view of Weill as a composer whose talents lay in his ability to capture the cynical and rather sleazy atmosphere of the Berlin of the Twenties and Thirties in tart little cabaret songs, is based almost entirely on the music of *The Threepenny Opera*, *Happy End* and, to a lesser extent, on the *Mahagonny Songspiel* – the three works in which the music most closely resembles that of cabaret songs and in which, for a variety of reasons, the moral stance of the authors is most easily ignored or misunderstood. Not only is the musical structure of all three works such as to encourage the performance of numbers as separate items removed from their dramatic context (so that the music of these works is best known as a series of unrelated songs) but, even within context, the social and moral implications of these works remain somewhat ambiguous. *Happy End*, for example, is most easily understood as a simple farce (Frederic Ewen, in his book on Brecht, dismisses the work as 'an unhappy farago' which 'were it not for the brilliant songs of Kurt Weill . . . might well be forgotten'[39]) while the libretto of *The Threepenny Opera* is, as all Brecht commentators have observed, so equivocal that the work can be easily accepted as little more than a brilliant *jeu d'esprit*.

The full-scale *Mahagonny* opera, on the other hand, presents a more difficult problem for those who wish to see Weill in this limited, and relatively comfortable, light, for in this piece the listener cannot avoid facing the issues which the work presents. The popular song style remains, but the individual numbers are far less easily divorced from their dramatic context than are the songs of *The Threepenny Opera* and this context, unlike that of the earlier work, is quite unambiguous in its moral and social position. The opera tells the story of the city of Mahagonny, a city of pleasure and of 'gin, whiskey, girls and boys', built to attract the gold flowing in from Alaska and the American west.

In Mahagonny everything is obtainable and everything is permissible if one has money. Act II of the opera illustrates some of the activities which make up the pleasurable existence of the inhabitants of Mahagonny: drinking, frequenting brothels, watching prize fights (the one shown on stage ends in the death of one of the combatants), eating until they kill themselves. Rape, murder and other crimes are regarded as trivial misdemeanours but lack of money is punishable by death. When, in the final Act of the work, one of the inhabitants can no longer pay his bills, he stands trial, is condemned and executed. God appears to the people of Mahagonny, but is unable to punish those who have already built a hell for themselves and the city is destroyed by flames.

Unlike *The Threepenny Opera*, *Mahagonny* is uncompromising in condemning the society which it presents. Ferocious both dramatically and musically, *Mahagonny* has none of the apparent bonhomie of the earlier work. It remains one of the most uncomfortable and disturbing of operas, as much because of Weill's oblique approach to his task as because of Brecht's text. In setting the scenes of self-indulgence in Act II and the horrifying final scenes of the opera to music of a deliberate banality, Weill was continuing that technique of distancing the listener by composing 'against', rather than 'with' the stage action that he had first employed in *The Protagonist*.

It is a technique that runs a high risk of defeating its own ends since the coming together of such horrifying stage action and such banal music can have an effect that is so shocking, and produce an alienation that is so brutal, that it may force the spectator to reject the work in equally aggressive terms. Perhaps no opera has aroused such hatred in its audience as has *Mahagonny*. The violent reaction of its earliest audience indicates not a misunderstanding of the piece but a clear understanding, and a rejection, of its message. Today, most people know *Mahagonny* and the 'popular' works of Weill through recorded, rather than staged, performances and it is, therefore, possible to ignore the oblique relationship between music and stage action. Divorced from its context, the music can be taken at its face value and its power reduced to manageable proportions. The present method of dealing with the almost unbearably painful images of *Mahagonny*, by regarding the music as a slightly cynical but amusing 'period piece', shows less understanding than was demonstrated by the work's first audiences.

I have earlier compared Weill's attitude to popular music with Stravinsky's attitude to the classical and baroque music which act as the models in his neo-classical works. Such a comparison seems fair when applied to the brilliant, often garish, music of *The Threepenny Opera*, *Happy End* and, to a lesser extent, *Mahagonny*, but it cannot be equally applied to the other works which Weill wrote between 1927 and 1935.

In *The Threepenny Opera* and *Happy End* Weill had used a simple sequence of cabaret songs as the vehicle for his newly established musical language. During the years that followed, the simple formal structures of these works disappeared, together with many of the more obvious external trappings of this new language, as Weill moved from an overtly 'jazzy', cabaret style to a less restrictive musical style.

The harmonic and many of the melodic features remain. These are the characteristic Weillian thumb-prints of the earlier works and it is not difficult to find passages in the later works that are directly reminiscent of the first Brecht-Weill pieces, as the following example demonstrates:

Ex 12 a Mahagonny Act II

b Seven Deadly Sins No 6 Unzucht

However, the more energetic jazz rhythms, the bright colours and what Drew has called 'the twentieth-century demotic expressions'[40] of popular music which are found in *The Threepenny Opera*, *Happy End* and parts of *Mahagonny* disappear. The move away from the overt cabaret, song style was a move towards a style that was more controlled, more flexible and at the same time less restricted. It was a move towards a style that retained the simple language and popular feeling of *The Threepenny Opera*, but was also capable of the austerity of *The Berlin Requiem*, the classical detachment of *Der Jasager* and the direct tragic statements of *Die Bürgschaft*. Above all, perhaps, it was a style that allowed for the development of larger musical structures.

In these post-*Threepenny Opera* and post-*Mahagonny* works the popular, jazz elements no longer form an implied 'background' against which the composed foreground operates. In works such as *The Seven Deadly Sins* the popular elements have become as much, and as natural, a part of Weill's style as was the folk element in the music of Haydn. To a large extent the movement towards this more flexible, more controlled style corresponds to a re-emergence of those neo-classical elements which had been present in Weill's earlier instrumental music. In fact, neo-classical influences had never completely disappeared from Weill's music (they can be seen, in particular, in *Mahagonny* in such things as the canon which accompanies the hurricane in Act II, in the chorale prelude which follows it and in the subtle polyphony of the 'Crane Duet') but had merely been obscured by the cabaret style of *Happy End* and *The Threepenny Opera*.

If Weill's instrumental works (other than the isolated Second Symphony) and the pre-Brecht operas can be considered as an attempt to fuse the two distinct influences of his early musical life – the expressionism of Mahler, Schoenberg and the late romantics and the neo-classicism of Busoni – into a unified musical language, then the works written after *Mahagonny* can be similarly viewed as an attempt to reconcile the new simpler and more popular language of the late 1920s with the neo-classicism of his earlier music.

The most obvious sign of Weill's move towards a more classical style is his gradual return to a more orthodox instrumental ensemble. The *Berlin Requiem* includes parts for banjo, guitar and two saxophones, but the saxophone is prominent in only one movement, and is elsewhere used as a member of a brass ensemble, while the banjo makes only a single appearance. The guitar, used as a popular rather than as a 'jazz' instrument, provides a simple chordal accompaniment to the ballade of the second movement, while the percussion consists only of timpani and, very sparingly employed, side drum and cymbals. By the time of *Der Jasager*, the saxophone and the banjo have disappeared and the piece has a purely Stravinskian ensemble.

Along with the polyphonic writing of these less specifically jazz-orientated ensembles there returns the polyphonic writing which was a feature of Weill's early instrumental music. Now it is a strong, muscular contrapuntal writing adapted to the demands of the new, popular language; Bachian figurations appear which, as in baroque music, are consistently and systematically exploited throughout a movement; baroque sequences and textures; baroque techniques (particularly canon which now forms the basis of almost all Weill's choruses) and a sense of rhythmic momentum and of thematic construction and extension that is clearly baroque in character.

On occasions the references to earlier music are quite specific. Both the text and the music of the finale number of *The Berlin Requiem* (the *Zweiter Bericht über den unbekannten Soldaten*), the opening of which is shown below, deliberately allude to the recitative style of the Bach Passions, an allusion that is intended to suggest a parallel between the subject matter of the *Requiem* and that of the Bach Passions.

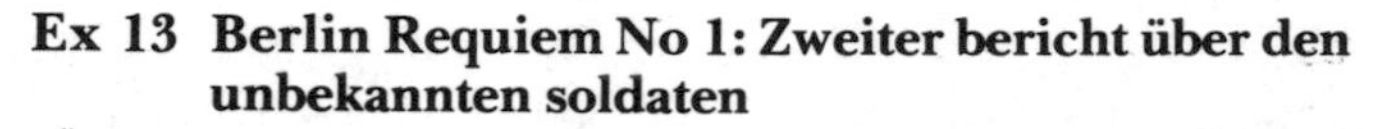

Ex 13 Berlin Requiem No 1: Zweiter bericht über den unbekannten soldaten

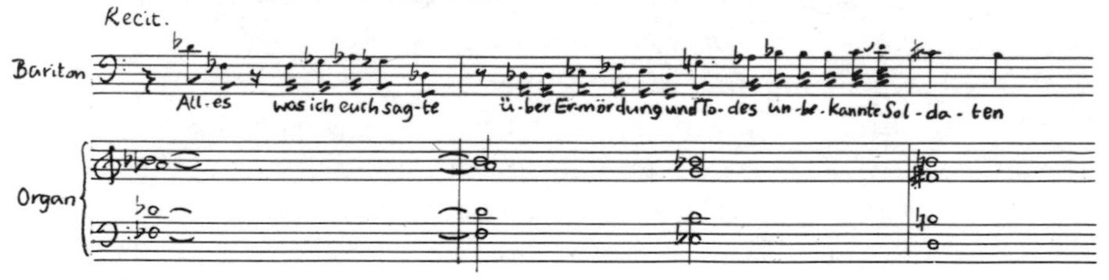

Such specific references are unusual, although they also occur in *Der Jasager* and the *Lindbergh Flight*; more important is the extent to which the neo-classical influence is completely absorbed into Weill's new popular, but now no longer specifically cabaret-style, language.

These other post-1927 European scores are marked by a classical sense of balance and by a technical and emotional restraint that is absent from the three better known Weill-Brecht works. In *Mahagonny* the savagery of the libretto is reflected in the ferocious bitterness of much of Weill's score. In *Die Bürgschaft*, on the other hand, the savagery is, as David Drew has pointed out, confined to the stage.[41]

Die Bürgschaft is about the way in which trust and friendship are corrupted by money and power. Act I of the opera is concerned with the subject on a personal level. Act II, in which the mythical country of the opera's setting is occupied by the forces of a totalitarian power, examines the relationship between the individual and the state. Act III portrays the effect which the new regime has on both the population as a whole and on the relationship between the two men whose story opened the opera. The final scene of the work, in which one man hands over his friend to be killed by the mob, is as horrifying and remorseless as anything to be found in opera. Yet, as Drew remarked, this act of 'consummate perfidiousness' is accompanied by music of an 'almost unbearable serenity.'[42] In *Der Jasager* a young boy joins an expedition through the mountains to the city so as to obtain medicine for his sick mother. In the course of the journey the boy himself falls ill, and, unable to continue, threatens the success of the expedition. He elects to die according to ancient custom by being thrown over the cliffs so that by his death the expedition can continue.

In both *Die Bürgschaft* and *Der Jasager* Weill's habitual practice of writing 'against' rather than 'with' the dramatic action – a technique which appeared in his first performed opera – is put to new ends. The sentencing and the execution of Jimmy Mahoney in *Mahagonny* is given an additional horror by being accompanied by music of a deliberate banality; the death of Johannes Mathes, at the end of *Die Bürgschaft*, and the sacrifice of the young boy in *Der Jasager* are accompanied by music which, by opposing the dramatic action, endistances and causes us to question, rather than experience, the morality of the violence shown on the stage; 'the music', as Weill himself observed in his comments on Busoni's *Doktor Faust*, 'leaves the interpretation of the outrageous events to the imagination of the listener and contents itself with a gesture of gentleness and freedom'.[43]

In both *Die Bürgschaft* and *Der Jasager* the characters are treated as stylized models, many of them are nameless (as in the expressionist drama of the period) and are simply identified by their function or status, with which (as in the Nō plays upon which Brecht based *Der Jasager*) they introduce themselves on their first appearance. The stylized, anti-naturalistic, nature of the two works is further emphasized by the music itself which, in both material and structure, recalls the conventions of baroque opera and oratorio. The final scene of *Die Bürgschaft*, for example, alternates *ritornelli* and episodes in the manner of a baroque concerto, while, in both works, the action is framed and punctuated by formal and dramatically static choruses. The chorus of *Der Jasager* is employed, in the manner of a Greek chorus, as a group which both participates in and, on other occasions, comments on or points out the moral of the stage action. In *Die Bürgschaft* the rôle of the chorus as disinterested commentator is emphasized physically by one chorus being on stage and a smaller, more important, 'commenting' chorus being seated, raised, in the orchestra pit or on the side of the stage.

Like Busoni, Weill believed that opera required a musical structure which existed independently of the dramatic action, a belief based – again like his teacher – on his experience of the operas of Mozart and Verdi. The formality of the musical design of *Die Bürgschaft* is not, therefore, an attempt to achieve the kind of fusion of 'abstract' musical forms and the dramatic demands of through-composed opera that Berg had achieved in *Wozzeck*. Like all Weill's work, from the *Threepenny Opera* onwards, *Die Bürgschaft* and *Der Jasager* are 'number' operas that totally reject the aesthetics and the techniques of the Wagnerian opera. Whole numbers and large, clearly defined, blocks of music (such as the choruses which frame Act I of *Die Bürgschaft*) reappear but such recurrences simply underline the formality of the musical and dramatic design. The Wagnerian *leitmotiv* has no place in Weill's dramatic works. Recurrent musical cells and shapes may appear, but these have a purely musical, rather than a 'literary', significance. The melodic pattern which opens *Der Jasager*, for example, is transformed to produce the theme of the chorus which greets the boy's decision to die; but the connection between the two musical ideas (which is stressed by the repetition of the opening section immediately after the related chorus) has no 'psychological' significance. When themes, rather than whole numbers, return they are isolated in such a way that the listener's attention is drawn to them; one such example is the passage, singled out by both its placing and orchestration, which ends numbers two and six and then becomes the basis of the seventh number of *The Seven Deadly Sins*.

As in Stravinsky's *Oedipus Rex*, with its equally objective commenting chorus, the symmetry and the formal design of these post-*Mahagonny* works is part of their stylized, monumental and deliberately ritualistic nature. Although Brecht dismissed *Die Bürgschaft* as 'bourgeois', the opera is as true to Brecht's conception of epic theatre, and as true to Weill's own belief in the necessity of evolving a new form of opera, as is the aggressive and more overtly iconoclastic *Mahagonny*.

Chapter 8
The American Works

To most admirers of Weill's European works, his output during the last fifteen years of his life comes as a profound shock. In these late works Weill the European intellectual, Weill the ironic observer of the political and social ills of his time, Weill the moralist – even Weill the composer with a limited but nonetheless individual and disturbing voice – seems to have disappeared. Instead, there emerges a picture of a composer willing to adopt the musical clichés of the Broadway musical and only too eager to embrace its commercial values. The picture also shows a composer happy to provide glossy, undistinguished music to libretti that are not simply apolitical but, in some cases, seem to condone all the attitudes that his earlier work critized. Inevitably, many people who value Weill's European works regard his American works with bewilderment, if not with horror.

The popular explanations of this apparent *volte-face*, of the 'problem' of Weill's American works, fall into two categories. Those who are interested in the European works primarily for literary, social or political reasons tend, as David Drew has pointed out,[1] to favour explanations that suggest that Weill could only compose when inspired by Brecht (or, on very rare occasions, some other forceful writer) and by the kind of social and political conditions found in the Germany of the inter-war years. Those who value Weill's earlier works for musical reasons find it impossible to believe that the sophisticated composer of *Mahagonny* could have employed the naive, and frequently sentimental, musical language of the American works with any degree of sincerity and, therefore, regard the American Weill as someone who betrayed his ideals by 'selling out'. The more charitable of these admirers may excuse this 'sell out' on the grounds that Weill had, after all, to make a living. The less charitable will regard him as a cynical opportunist or as someone corrupted by the financial rewards available to anyone willing, and able, to produce a slick commercial product. Amongst the latter group may be numbered Otto Klemperer who, when asked 'why Weill went to pieces as a composer in America' replied: 'He was very interested in money, that's the reason. He got too involved in American show business and all the terrible people in it.'[2]

None of these explanations does justice to Weill or shows any understanding of the complicated process by means of which the European Weill was transformed into the rich and famous Broadway composer of the late 1940s – a process in which Weill's social and musical beliefs, his complex psychological make-up and the historic events of the period all play a part.

I have already discussed the extent to which Brecht's aims have been mistakenly assumed to be those of Weill also. Weill's main concerns were always social, humanistic and musical, rather than directly political. Unlike Eisler, Weill was never willing to subjugate his musical ideals to the expression of a clear and unambiguous political message and, indeed, the break between Weill and Brecht came at the point at which Brecht's political ideas began to interfere with what Weill regarded as the musical necessities of the work.

Once the true nature of Weill's aims is recognized it becomes possible to see that, far from betraying his ideals, Weill pursued both his musical and social aims in these American works with what, given the new cultural environment within which he was working, was remarkable single-mindedness.

Weill's output in America can be conveniently divided into three groups, each group covering a period of five years. The first group of works, written between 1935 and 1940, includes *Der Weg der Verheissung*, *Johnny Johnstone*, and his first Broadway musical, *Knickerbocker Holiday*. The second, covering the period 1941-45, consists of *Lady in the Dark*, *One Touch of Venus* and *The Firebrand of Florence*. The final group covers the last five years of his life and includes the folk opera, *Down in the Valley*, *Street Scene*, *Love Life* and *Lost in the Stars*.

To those familiar with Weill's European works, the second of these groups is, at least in terms of subject matter, the most problematic. Pure, commercial Broadway shows, it is difficult to detect any social or humanistic concerns behind the stories of *Lady in the Dark* (which deals with the psychological problems and fantasies of the editoress of a fashion magazine), *One Touch of Venus* (in which a statue of Venus comes to life and falls in love with a barber) or in *The Firebrand of Florence* (about Benvenuto Cellini's attempts to win the hand of the girl he loves). These three works are exceptional, however, and all Weill's other American works deal with social and moral subjects that reflect concerns as topical and relevant to the American audiences of the period as were those of the earlier works to his European audience. The theme of war, for example, is dealt with in the anti-militaristic *Johnny Johnstone*; racial tensions in *Lost in the Stars*; tenement life in *Street Scene* and politics in *Knickerbocker Holiday*. Certainly Weill never again found a librettist as poetic, as dramatically skilled or as hard-hitting as Brecht. Nonetheless, if the handling of these social themes seems timid, rather naive and often peripheral to the more obviously commercial aspects of the story, we must recognize that, given the state of the commercial Broadway theatre of the time, even to tackle such subjects was a brave innovation.

The simple, popular style which Weill had adopted in the European works of the mid-1920s had been an attempt to achieve a musical language which would be immediately comprehensible to a large number of people, which would, in Weill's own words, 'enable meaningful things to be said with the simplest, most inconspicuous of means'[3] and which would enable the 'new opera' to reach a 'new public'. In the radical and experimental atmosphere of the Germany of the inter-war years, it had been possible for the development of the new language and new forms to take place within the confines of the established opera houses and the serious theatre. In the United States Weill found himself faced with a culture which did not allow for such possibilities. The serious 'play with music' – the form which, well-established in Europe, gave rise to *The Threepenny Opera* and *Der Silbersee* – was almost unknown in America, while American opera houses (of which, compared with Germany, there existed a mere handful) catered exclusively for one particular, élite section of the population.

In *Down in the Valley*, a work intended for performances by non-professional groups, the preface in the score says:

> [it] can be performed wherever a chorus, a few singers and a few actors are available. The physical production can be as simple as a 'dramatic' concert performance where the principal act their scenes in front of the chorus without any help of scenery. If scenery is used it should consist of some

> simply painted frames indicating the place . . . the leading parts should provide good training for the specific type of singing actor who has become such an important asset of the musical theatre.

This work represented one attempt to reach a wider popular audience. If *Down in the Valley* has behind it none of the didactic political intentions of a Lehrstück such as *Der Jasager*, its intentions of providing some kind of musical training are similar, and are directly in line with the aims of the Gebrauchsmusik of the Germany of the 1920s. The extent to which *Down in the Valley* succeeded in achieving its aims can be judged by the fact that the piece received over 1,600 productions (and some 6,000 performances) in the first nine years of its life.

Such things as *Down in the Valley* and the 'Lunchtime' shows, in which Weill took such pleasure, were, however, a response to a specialized and specific social demand. To reach a truly popular audience Weill had to work within the mainstream of the American music theatre and this, inevitably, meant the Broadway musical.

'A composer must know for whom he is composing',[4] Weill observed, and in order to reach an American public Weill had to find a new, and specifically American, musical language which would be as generally comprehensible as had been the language of his later European works. During the period from 1941-45 this language was that of the Broadway musical; after 1945, and after the disastrous reception of *The Firebrand of Florence*, the language was more consciously based on the melodic and rhythmic inflections of American folk music and on the popular music of the streets, rather than on commercial popular music. Langston Hughes, the black American poet who wrote the lyrics of *Street Scene*, has described how Weill went with him to hear authentic blues numbers in different parts of Harlem and studied American children's games and songs in order to achieve a 'national idiom' that would be understood by the American people.[5] In the obituary of Weill which appeared in the *New York Herald Tribune* on 9 April 1950, Virgil Thomson acknowledged Weill's success in creating such a national idiom, saying of *Down in the Valley* that, 'it speaks an American musical dialect that Americans can accept'.

If Broadway seemed to offer Weill the chance of reaching a popular audience it also, more than anywhere else, seemed to offer the possibility of creating both new forms of music-theatre and large-scale musical structures approaching those of opera.

A few weeks after his arrival in the United States, Weill attended the dress rehearsal of Gershwin's *Porgy and Bess*. According to Weill himself, the experience made him realize that, 'the American theatre was well on the way to the more integrated form of musical theatre that we had begun to attempt in Europe. That gave me the courage to start work on a serious musical play for the American stage – *Johnny Johnson*.'[6] However, Lotte Lenya's memories of the occasion suggest that Gershwin's achievement in *Porgy* had a more far-reaching effect on Weill: 'He listened very closely and he said, "you know, it is possible to write an opera for Broadway".' From that point onwards, said Lenya, Weill was, 'always consciously working towards an opera'.[7] There can be little doubt that Weill, who had urged the necessity for a 'new type of opera' in the Germany of the 1920s, felt the need for a similarly new type of American opera. Moreover, it was clear to him that such a new type of opera could not develop in the United States within the confines of the opera house. As early as 1937, shortly after the production of *Johnny Johnson* and before his first Broadway musical, Weill had declared his belief that:

> If there will ever be anything like an American opera, it is bound to come out of Broadway. To start a new movement of American musical theater, you cannot go to the Metropolitan. They haven't got the audience. Broadway represents the living theater in this country and American opera, as I imagine it, should be part of the living theater. Opera has lost contact with the theater and leads the existence of a museum piece, toilsomely preserved by its devotees.[8]

Few of Weill's American works were pat 'formula', 'sure-fire', musicals. Within the context of the commercial Broadway musical theatre both the subjects and their musical treatment were unusually adventurous. There were, for example, few precedents within the tradition of the musical for such things as the 'Greek' chorus of *Lost in the Stars*, the confining of the music of *Lady in the Dark* to the dream sequences (in themselves miniature, self-contained operas) or the ensembles of *Street Scene*.

It is difficult today to realize the extent to which a work such as *Street Scene* differed from the other, more commercial musicals of its time. Contemporary critics, however, were in no doubt that the work, with its complex ensembles and large musical structures, its single set and simple costumes, its lack of dancers, chorus, comedians and lavish production numbers represented a step towards 'a significantly American opera'. During the last five years of his life Weill seems to have been more and more consciously attempting to create an indigenous operatic tradition based on the classics of American literature. At the time of his death he was working on a version of Mark Twain's *Huckleberry Finn* and Lotte Lenya remembers finding on his desk a list of equally 'classic' subjects including *Gone with the Wind* and Melville's *Moby Dick* that Weill was considering using as the bases of future works.

In his *New York Herald Tribune* obituary Virgil Thomson referred to Weill's attempts to found an American operatic tradition and described him as, 'a workman who might have bridged for us the gap between grand opera and the singspiel'.[9] Five years later, the critic Gilbert Chase acknowledged the stature of Weill's achievements in the late works, saying that Weill had given the American theatre 'works that transcend the level of popular entertainment'.[10] That we, today, find it difficult to accept the folksiness, the sentimentality and the rather self-conscious 'messages' of these late works may simply indicate that the spirit which these pieces embody no longer forms a part of our mental attitude: the cynicism of the European works is more in tune with our way of looking at the world than is the innocence and naivety of the American works.

It is easy to overlook, or ignore, how consistent and how brave, given the cultural context, were Weill's attempts to retain his integrity. The tenacity with which he continued, in these American works, to pursue his life-long musical, social and humanistic beliefs gives the lie to the idea that the American Weill betrayed the ideals which he had promoted in his earlier European works. Weill's belief in the necessity for a new form of opera never changed; nor his belief that this new opera should reach a new public. Only his ideas about the way in which these ends were to be achieved had undergone a transformation.

There remains, however, what, to anyone whose interest in Weill is primarily musical, are the most perplexing and problematic aspects of his American music. That most of the American works are of a lower musical standard – often of a much lower standard – than Weill's European works is, I think, undeniable. Comparing Weill's

European and American works, David Drew, the most perceptive and sympathetic of commentators on Weill, has said; 'I know of no composer, indeed no creative artist of any kind, in whose work there is so great a gulf between the best and the worst',[11] and has observed of *Down in the Valley* that 'even the technique is deficient; shoddy modulations abound, simple tunes are decked out with meaningless counterpoints, empty *ostinati* do service of real invention.'[12]

Equally, and perhaps more, disconcerting than the standard of the music, is the nature of the change in Weill's musical language in the works written in the last fifteen years of his life. The change of style which took place in Weill's music during the 1920s is startling but not only is it possible to see the links between the atonal Weill of the Violin Concerto and the popular, jazz-based Weill of *The Threepenny Opera*, it is also possible to understand the changes in his style in terms of the more general artistic and musical trends in Europe of that period. As I have tried to show, the popular style of Weill's later European music has its roots in the European tradition within which he grew up, and in the developments within that tradition which were taking place during his formative years.

If Weill's works from the years 1927 to 1935 represent an extension – albeit an extension in a surprising and unpredictable direction – of the European tradition, the American works seem to represent a complete rejection of this tradition; a denial, rather than a development, of Weill's earlier style. The nature of the American commercial theatre and the desire to write for an American audience in a musical language which it would understand, could explain a change in the more superficial aspects of Weill's musical style; they cannot explain a change as profound as that which actually took place.

Despite Drew's remarks on the technical weakness of *Down in the Valley*, the American pieces are rarely less than the works of a skilled and totally professional craftsman. Even at their best, however, they are works of a kind that could have been written by a number of competent Broadway composers. In these works the individual voice of the European Weill seems to have disappeared into an anonymous stylistic greyness.

Since Weill, as reticent as ever about his inner thoughts and feelings, left no indication as to why this profound change in his language took place, one can only surmise the deep psychological and personal factors which led him to cultivate this apparently deliberate anonymity. Some attempt at this is necessary if one is to approach an understanding of Weill's American career.

It is difficult to overestimate the profound effect which emigration had on those forced by circumstances to leave Germany in the 1930s. Despite his total silence on the subject, the extremity of Weill's response is a measure of the depth of the psychological and emotional effect which the experience had on him.

We know from Lotte Lenya that, once in America, Weill never spoke German again – even his dying words were in English.[13] Similarly, we know that he refused to have anything to do with his fellow refugees, even with those, such as Hindemith, who had previously been amongst his closest personal friends. Lotte Lenya has said:

> The old timers were always talking about the past, they would always talk about how marvellous it had been in Berlin . . . Weill didn't want to have anything to do with refugees. He never saw any of them again. Never . . . Kurt never wanted to look back.[14]

Lenya has suggested that Weill's refusal to speak his native language or talk about his earlier life came about because he 'was always looking ahead', but there can be little doubt that it was also a part of Weill's reaction to the experience of emigration. Driven from his homeland, Weill rejected everything that that homeland represented.

It was not by chance that the various attempts by Adorno, Aufricht and others to revive Weill's European works or to suggest new projects on which Weill and Brecht might once again collaborate, came to nothing. Virgil Thomson remembers that, soon after Weill and Lotte Lenya had arrived in the United States, he and a number of other people:

> thought that it would be good to produce in Hartford Weill's German opera made with Brecht, *Mahagonny*. We took Weill there to see the theatre, and I even played through the score with him for setting tempos. But quietly the project was dropped and one came to understand that Weill's working association with Bertolt Brecht . . . was to be buried. And buried it remained until his death.[15]

Thomson suggests that Weill wanted to hide 'a possibly Communist-tainted past'. It seems more likely, however, that Weill simply wanted, as Lenya has remarked, 'to forget everything German'.

In any event, the Germany that Weill had known had disappeared.

In May 1938, while Weill was working on *Knickerbocker Holiday*, his first Broadway musical, the scores of his European pieces were being displayed in Dusseldorf as part of the Nazi Ministry of Propaganda's exhibition of 'Debased Music'. *Magna Carta*, Weill's declaration of human rights, was written in the early months of 1940, by which time the French and British governments had declared war and the German military high command was preparing for its spectacular spring offensive. By May 1940 the Germans had overrun all the countries to the west of them and Weill's Europe – his background and his roots, the culture which had formed him, everything that he had stood for and believed in – had been destroyed.

Rejected by the society within which he had been brought up, betrayed by the culture of which he had regarded himself a part, the American Weill had to re-establish not only his career but his very identity. The use of ancient Jewish modes in *Der Weg der Verheissung*, the occasional pieces written to celebrate the founding of the state of Israel, and the liturgical setting of *Kiddush* for cantor, mixed chorus and organ, demonstrate the extent to which exile and the experiences which led to it, forced Weill, as it did many other Jews, to recognize and reassess their identity as members of the Jewish race.

Alongside the psychological rejection of everything to do with Germany, and the recognition of his racial identity, Weill also had to assert his new national identity as an American. Following the publication of a review of *Street Scene* in February 1947, Weill wrote to *Life* magazine to complain of their description of him as a German composer:

> Although I was born in Germany I do not consider myself a 'German composer'. The Nazis obviously do not consider me as such either and I left their country (an arrangement which suited both me and my rulers admirably) in 1933. I am an American citizen and during my dozen years in this country have composed exclusively for the American stage . . . I would appreciate your straightening out your readers on this matter.[16]

Weill wanted, Lenya has said, 'to absorb America; he really wanted to get into America'[17] and to become a true American, not an American 'simply on paper'. Weill could only establish his new identity as an American citizen, as opposed to an expatriate German, by adopting the standards and the values of his new home.

It is not, perhaps, surprising that Weill threw himself with such eagerness into helping the American war effort (it is significant that the only settings of the German language which he composed while in the United States were specifically written for propaganda broadcasts) nor that, following the end of the war and the disastrous reception of *The Firebrand of Florence*, he should have become even more determined to submerge himself in the culture of his new country and create a truly 'American' music for the American people.

If this adoption of American values necessitated the renunciation of his earlier musical language and of the European culture which that language represented, if his rejection of 'everything German' necessitated the denial of his previous musical identity and what seems to have been the deliberate cultivation of an anonymous 'American' style, then these were the prices that Weill was prepared to pay.

Perhaps some insight into Weill's attitudes during the last fifteen years of his life can be gained by seeing the way in which his compatriot George Grosz responded to the cultural and social trauma of emigration. In her book on Grosz, Beth Irwin Lewis observes:

> He did not find paradise in America, though he tried desperately hard to become a complete American. He was determined not to live like an exile, living in the past and waiting to return to Germany. He intended to shed his German identity and sink his roots into the new land. He threw himself with enthusiasm into becoming a practical, money-making American but the ties with Germany were too strong. He wrote some time later, 'I really haven't brought it off. I can never become a genuine American. Thus, I am, after all, nothing more than – yes, a demoralized and forgotten German.'[18]

In both his art and his outer life Weill shed his German identity more successfully than did Grosz; indeed, in his American works Weill actually demonstrated the gradual shedding of his old identity and the acquisition of a new one in the clearest way available to a composer. Whether Weill, like Grosz, felt demoralized, whether he too felt that he had not 'brought it off' is something that he never revealed but he, at least, was not a 'forgotten German'. As Lotte Lenya has remarked, 'He had success all his life. One cannot say, in his case, that when he died, he died misunderstood.'[19]

There is, nonetheless, a bitter irony in the fact that Weill's greatest

American success came a few years after his death, not with a work written in his later 'American' style but with a piece from that period of his life that he had tried to forget. When *The Threepenny Opera* was revived at an off-Broadway theatre in 1954 it ran for a record breaking 2,707 performances – a run that surpassed not only the runs of Weill's own Broadway shows but also the runs of such legendary musicals as *Oklahoma*, *The Sound of Music*, *South Pacific* and, as a final irony, the Weill-Brecht inspired *Cabaret*.

CHRONOLOGICAL LIST OF WORKS

The following list of works includes all Weill's major compositions, whether published or unpublished. Excluded are the many works which Weill began and never completed, the numerous individual songs and the various arrangements which Weill made of his own and other composers' pieces.

Pre 1919	*Schilflieder* song cycle (unpublished) Piano pieces (unpublished)
1919	*Die Weise von Liebe und Tod des Cornets Christopher Rilke,* symphonic poem for orchestra (unpublished)
1919-20	String Quartet in B minor (unpublished) Sonata for 'Cello and Piano (unpublished) *Nina der Lenclos*, opera in one act (unpublished, lost) *Das Hohe Lied*, opera in one act (unpublished, lost) *Shulamith*, oratorio (unpublished)
1921	Symphony No. 1 (Universal Edition, Vienna)
1922	*Divertimento* for orchestra and male chorus (unpublished) *Sinfonia Sacra* op 6 (unpublished) *Die Zaubernacht*, ballet for children (unpublished)
1923	*Recordare* (unpublished) String Quartet op 8 (Universal Edition, Vienna) *Quodlibet* op 9 (Universal Edition, Vienna) *Frauentanz* op 10 for voice and instruments (Universal Edition, Vienna) *Stundenbuch* for voice and orchestra (unpublished, lost)
1924	Concerto for violin and wind instruments (Universal Edition, Vienna) *Der Protagonist*, opera in one act on a libretto by Georg Kaiser (vocal score: Universal Edition, Vienna) *Der neue Orpheus*, cantata on a text by Ivan Goll (vocal score: Universal Edition, Vienna)
1926	*Royal Palace*, opera in one act on a libretto by Ivan Goll (vocal score: Universal Edition, Vienna) *Herzog von Gothland*, incidental music for a radio play (unpublished) *Na und . . .*, comic opera (unpublished, lost)
1927	*Gustav III*, incidental music for a stage play (unpublished) *Der Zar lässt sich photographieren*, one-act opera on a libretto by Georg Kaiser (vocal score: Universal Edition, Vienna) *Mahagonny Songspiel*, text by Bertolt Brecht (Universal Edition, Vienna) *Vom Tod im Wald*, for bass and wind instruments. Text by Bertolt Brecht (unpublished)
1928	*Konjunktur*, incidental music for a stage play (unpublished) *Katalaunische Schlacht*, incidental music for a stage play (unpublished) *Der Dreigroschenoper* (The Threepenny Opera), a play with music. Text by Bertolt Brecht (Universal Edition, Vienna)

	Kleine Dreigroschenmusik for wind (Universal Edition, Vienna) *Das Berliner Requiem*, cantata on poems by Bertolt Brecht (vocal score: Universal Edition, Vienna)
1929	*Der Lindberghflug* (Der Ozeanflug), radio cantata on a text by Bertolt Brecht (vocal score: Universal Edition, Vienna) *Aufstieg und Fall der Stadt Mahagonny* (The Rise and Fall of the City of Mahagonny), opera in three acts on a libretto by Bertolt Brecht (vocal score: Universal Edition, Vienna) *Happy End*, comedy with music on a text by Elisabeth Hauptmann and Dorothy Lane. Songs by Bertolt Brecht (Universal Edition, Vienna) *Petroleuminseln*, incidental music for a stage play (unpublished)
1930	*Der Jasager*, school opera in two acts on a libretto by Bertolt Brecht (Universal Edition, Vienna) *Mann ist Mann*, incidental music for a play (lost)
1931	*Die Bürgschaft*, opera in three acts on a libretto by Caspar Neher (vocal score: Universal Edition, Vienna)
1932	*Der Silbersee*, a play with music by Georg Kaiser (vocal score: Universal Edition, Vienna)
1933	*Der Sieben Todsünden der Kleinbürger* (The Seven Deadly Sins of the Bourgeoisie), ballet by Bertolt Brecht (Universal Edition, Vienna)
1934	Symphony No. 2 (Schotts Söhne, Mainz) *Marie Galante*, a play with music by Jacques Deval (songs published by Heugel et Cie, Paris)
1935	*Der Kuhhandel*, comic operetta on a play by Robert Vaubery (two songs published by Chappell and Co., New York) *The Eternal Road*, dramatic oratorio on a text by Franz Werfel (vocal score: Heugel et Cie, Paris)
1936	*Johnny Johnson*, a musical play by Paul Green (vocal score: Samuel French, New York)
1938	*Knickerbocker Holiday*, musical comedy by Maxwell Anderson (vocal score: De Sylva, Brown and Henderson)
1939	*Railroads on Parade*, dramatic pageant (unpublished) *Ballad of Magna Carta*, cantata (vocal score: Chappell and Co., New York)
1941	*Lady in the Dark*, a musical play by Moss Hart, lyrics by Ira Gershwin (Chappell and Co., New York)
1942	*Three Walt Whitman Songs* (Chappell and Co., New York)
1943	*One Touch of Venus*, a musical comedy by S J Perelman and Ogden Nash (songs published by Chappell and Co., New York)
1945	*The Firebrand of Florence*, musical play by Edwin Justus Meyer, lyrics by Ira Gershwin (songs published by Chappell and Co., New York)

1946	*Kiddush* for cantor, chorus and organ (published in 'Synagogue music by contemporary composers', Schirmer, New York)
1947	*Street Scene*, an American opera by Elmer Rice, lyrics by Langston Hughes (Chappell and Co., New York)
1948	*Down in the Valley*, a folk opera by Arnold Sundgard (vocal score: Schirmer, New York) *Love Life*, a vaudeville by Alan J Lerner (songs published by Chappell and Co., New York)
1949	*Lost in the Stars*, a musical tragedy based on Alan Paton's 'Cry, the Beloved Country' by Maxwell Anderson (vocal score: Chappell and Co., New York)
1950	*Huckleberry Finn*, unfinished musical play by Maxwell Anderson (five completed songs published by Chappell and Co., New York)

DISCOGRAPHY

At present most of the recordings of Weill's music are of the most popular of the works which he wrote in collaboration with Bertolt Brecht; there are, therefore, no available recordings of *Die Bürgschaft*, *The Protagonist*, *Der neue Orpheus*, *Royal Palace*, *Der Zar lässt sich photographieren*, *Der Jasager* or *Der Ozeanflug*.

Of the popular Brecht-Weill works there exist complete, but rather old, recordings of *The Rise and Fall of the City of Mahagonny* (R77341) *The Threepenny Opera* (R78279) and *Happy End* (R73453) conducted by W. Bruckner-Ruggenberg and with a cast that includes Lotte Lenya. There are also fascinating historic recordings (made in 1930) of excerpts from these three works sung by the original cast, played by the Lewis-Ruth Band and conducted by the original conductor Theo Mackeben on AJ 641911.

The most representative selection of Weill's European music is to be found on the Deutsche Grammophon recording of the London Sinfonietta conducted by David Atherton. This boxed set includes the Violin Concerto, the *Berlin Requiem*, *Vom Tod im Wald*, the *Kleine Dreigroschenmusik*, the first Pantomime from *The Protagonist* and the *Mahagonny Songspiel* (DGG 2740-153). A further performance of the *Mahagonny Songspiel* with the Jerusalem Symphony Orchestra conducted by Lukas Foss can be found on Turnabout TV 34675. A recording of *The Seven Deadly Sins* sung by Lotte Lenya and conducted by W. Bruckner-Ruggenberg can be found on R73657.

A recent recording of the New York City Opera's version of *Der Silbersee* appears on Nonesuch DB 79003.

Of Weill's early, that is to say pre-Brecht works, there are recordings of the *Quodlibet* op 9 (played by the Westphalian Symphony Orchestra conducted by Siegfried Landau on TV 37124) and the First Symphony (in two performances: one by the BBC Symphony Orchestra conducted by Bertini on ZRG 755, one by the Leipzig Gewandhaus under Edo de Wart on 6500-642) in addition to the Sinfonietta performance of the Violin Concerto mentioned above. Both recordings of the First Symphony couple it with performances of the Second Symphony by the same artists.

Of Weill's American works there are in existence old, in most cases the original, recordings of *One Touch of Venus* (with Mary Martin, conducted by Maurice Abravanel on Decca DL 79122) and *Lost in the Stars* (DL71920). Selections from *Lady in the Dark*, sung by Gertrude Lawrence, are coupled with a version of *Down in the Valley* conducted by Peter Adler on RCA LPV-503. A complete performance of *Down in the Valley*, conducted by Maurice Levine, can be found on Decca DL 74239.

BIBLIOGRAPHY

BOOKS

Appignanesi, L *The Cabaret* (Studio Vista, London 1975)
Atkinson, B *Broadway* (Cassell, London 1971)
Bullock, A *Hitler: A Study in Tyranny* (Penguin Books, London 1969)
Carter, E *The Writings of Elliot Carter* (ed. by E and K Stone) (Indiana University Press, Bloomington/London 1977)
Dent, E J *Ferruccio Busoni* (E Eulenberg, London-reprinted 1974)
Drew, D (ed.) *Über Kurt Weill* (Suhrkamp taschenbuch, Frankfurt 1975)
Drummond, A *American Opera Libretti* (Scarecrow Press, New Jersey 1973)
Eisler, Hanns *A Rebel in Music* (ed. M Gruber) (Seven Seals Publications, Berlin 1978)
Ewen, F *Bertolt Brecht* (Calder & Boyars, London 1967)
Eyck, E *A History of the Weimar Republic* (Oxford University Press, Harvard University Press 1964)
Friedrich, O *Before the Deluge* (Michael Joseph, London 1974)
Gay, P *Weimar Culture* (Penguin Books, London 1974)
Gershwin, I *Lyrics On Several Occasions* (Hamish Hamilton, London 1977)
Green, S *The Encyclopedia of Musicals* (Cassell, London 1977)
Hamilton, George Heard *Painting and Sculpture in Europe 1880-1940* (Penguin Books, London 1972)
Heinsheimer, H W *Fanfare for Two Pigeons* (Doubleday & Co., New York 1951)
Heinsheimer, H W *Menagerie in F Sharp* (T V Boardman & Co., New York 1949)
Hitchcock, Henry Russell *Architecture: Nineteenth and Twentieth Centuries* (Penguin Books, London 1971)
Innes, C D *Erwin Piscator's Political Theatre* (Cambridge University Press, 1972)
Jackson, A *The Book of Musicals* (Mitchell Beazley, London 1979)
Kemp, Ian *Paul Hindemith* (Oxford University Press, 1970)
Marx, H (ed.) *Weill-Lenya* (Goethe House, New York 1976)
Milhaud, D *Notes without Music* (Alfred A Knopf, New York 1952)
Slonimsky, N *Music Since 1900* (Cassell, London 1971 – 4th edition)
Thomson, V *Virgil Thomson* (Weidenfeld & Nicholson, London 1967)
Walter, B *Theme and Variations* (trans. J A Galston) (Hamish Hamilton, London 1947)
Weill, K *Ausgewählte Schriften* (ed. D Drew) (Suhrkamp Verlag, Franfurt 1975)
Willett, J *The Theatre of Erwin Piscator* (Eyre Methuen, London 1978)
Willett, J (ed.) *Brecht on Theatre* (Eyre Methuen, London 1978)
Zweig, S *The World of Yesterday* (Cassell, London 1943)

BIBLIOGRAPHY

ARTICLES

Adam, P 'Lotte Lenya: September Song' *The Listener* 24 May 1979, pp 707-9
Aufricht, E J 'Die Moritāt vom Mackie Messer' *Melos* November 1966, pp 359-63
Branscombe, P 'Brecht, Weill and *Mahagonny*' *Musical Times* No 102, August 1961, p 483
Downes, O 'Musical Sociology' *New York Times* 4 April 1954, sect. 2, p 7
Drew, D 'Brecht versus opera' *Score* No 23, July 1958, pp 7-10
Drew, D 'Happy End' notes to CBS record 73463
Drew, D 'The History of *Mahagonny*' *Musical Times* January 1963, pp 18-24
Drew, D 'Kurt Weill', notes to DGG record 2740 153
Drew, D 'Kurt Weill and his critics' *The Times Literary Supplement* 3 and 10 October 1975, pp 1142-1198
Drew, D 'Music Theatre in the Weimar Republic' *Proceedings of the Royal Musical Association, vol 88 1962*
Drew, D 'Topicality and the Universal' *Music and Letters* No 39, July 1958, pp 242-55
Drew, D 'Two Weill Scores' *Musical Times* No 107, September 1966, pp 797-8
Drew, D 'Symphony 1' preface to published score, Universal Edition, Vienna
Drew, D 'Symphony 2' preface to published score, Universal Edition, Vienna
Drew, D 'Weill's School Opera' *Musical Times* No 106, December 1964, pp 897-9
East, L 'A Festival of Weill' *Music & Musicians* March 1977, pp 36-40
Engelmann, H U 'Kurt Weill-heute' *Darmstadter Beträge* No 3, 1960, pp 87-95
Helm, E 'Weill's *Bürgschaft*' *Saturday Review* No 40, 16 November 1957, pp 35-9
Hewes, H 'The Theatre' *Saturday Review* No 55, 6 May 1972, pp 64-5
Horowitz, J 'Lotte Lenya recalls Weill's "Street Scene"' *New York Times* 26 October, 1979
Kemp, I 'Harmony in Weill: Some Observations' *Tempo* 10 April, 1973, pp 11-15
Kemp, I 'Symphony 1' notes to record ZRG 755
Koegler, H 'Kurt Weills amerikanische Bühnenwerke' *Melos* March 1956, pp 67-70
Lenya, L 'In conversation with Steven Paul', notes to DGG 2740 153
Padmore, E 'Kurt Weill' *Music & Musicians* October 1972, pp 34-40
Redlich, H 'Kurt Weill' *Music Review* 11 August 1950, p 208
Reinhardt, M 'Brecht und das musikalisches Theatre' *Musik und Bild* No 3 November 1971, pp 522-5
Weill, K 'Aktuelles Theater' *Melos* 37, July/August 1970, pp 276-7
Weinraub, B 'Lenya on Weill: The Memory Lingers On' *New York Times* 25 October, 1964

Other Sources:
For information on Weill's American career the following are useful sources:
Chronologies in the New York Goethe House's 'Weill-Lenya' produced as a booklet to accompany their 1976 exhibition in New York.
Kowalke's notes for the booklet of the 1979 New York City Opera production of *Street Scene*.

NOTES

CHAPTER 1

1 see Drew, David 'Introduction and Notes' in booklet accompanying the Weill Symphony No 1 (Argo ZRG 755)
2 *ibid.*
3 see Kastner, Rudolf *Weill und Busoni* reprinted in Drew, David (ed.) *Über Kurt Weill* (Suhrkamp Taschenbuch, Frankfurt 1975, p. 11)
4 see Drew, David 'First Symphony' in notes accompanying the Weill Symphony No 1 (Argo ZRG 755)
5 *ibid.*
6 Stuckenschmidt, H H *Ferruccio Busoni* (Calder & Boyars, London 1967, p. 178)
7 Dent, E J *Busoni* (E. Eulenberg, London 1974, p. 127)
8 Weill quoted in Stuckenschmidt, *op.cit.*, p. 196
9 *ibid.*
10 Wasserman, Jacob quoted in Stuckenschmidt, *op.cit.*, p. 63
11 Selden-Goth, Gisella quoted in Stuckenschmidt, *ibid.*, p. 64
12 Dent, E J *op.cit.*, p. 287
13 Kastner, Rudolf *op.cit.*, p. 10
14 see Drew, David 'First Symphony', *op.cit*
15 Heinsheimer, Hans *Menagerie in F Sharp* (T V Boardman & Co., New York 1949, p. 131)
16 *ibid.*
17 see Drew, David (ed.) *Vorwort* in *Kurt Weill: Ausgewählte Schriften* (Suhrkamp Verlag, Frankfurt 1975, p. 13)
18 Weill, Kurt *Der Protagonist* in *Kurt Weill; Ausgewählte Schriften, op.cit.*, p. 53
19 Lenya, Lotte 'In Conversation with Steven Paul' in booklet accompanying Kurt Weill, London Sinfonietta, DGG 2740-153
20 compiled from Lenya, Lotte *ibid.*, and Lenya, Lotte 'September Song' (*The Listener*, 24 May 1979, p. 707)
21 Lenya, Lotte, *ibid.*
22 Weill, Kurt *Meine Frau* in *Kurt Weill: Ausgewählte Schriften, op.cit.*, p. 9

CHAPTER 2

1 Zweig, Stefan *The World of Yesterday* (Cassell, London 1943, p. 298)
2 Walter, Bruno *Theme and Variations* (Hamish Hamilton, London 1947, p. 276)
3 Zweig, Stefan *op.cit.*, p. 312
4 Walter, Bruno *op.cit.*, p. 277
5 Zweig, Stefan *op.cit.*, p. 311
6 Bullock, Alan *Hitler: A Study in Tyranny* (Penguin Books, London 1969, pp. 90-1)
7 Zweig, Stefan *op.cit.*, p. 301
8 *ibid.*, p. 292
9 *ibid.*, p. 313
10 Kessler, Count Harry *Tagebücher 1918-1937* quoted in Friedrich, Otto *Before The Deluge* (Michael Joseph, London 1974, pp. 37, 51)
11 Zweig, Stefan *op.cit.*, p. 361
12 *ibid.*, p. 361
13 Lenya, Lotte 'In Conversation with Steven Paul' in programme booklet accompanying Kurt Weill, London Sinfonietta (DGG 2740-153, p. 8)

14 Walter, Bruno *op.cit.*, p. 296
15 Hulsenbeck, Richard *Die Dadaistische Bewegung. Eine Selbstbiographie*, quoted in Raabe, P *The Era of German Expressionism* (Calder & Boyars, London 1974, p. 352)
16 Piscator, Erwin 'The Proletarian Theatre: Its Fundamental Principles and Tasks'. First published in *Die Gegner*, October 1920; reprinted in translation in *Culture and Agitation: Theatre Documents*, Howard, Roger (ed.) (Action Books, London 1972, p. 42)
17 Hulsenbeck, Richard *op.cit.*, p. 352
18 Hindemith, Paul quoted in Kemp, Ian *Paul Hindemith* (Oxford University Press, 1970)
19 Eisler, Hanns 'Our Revolutionary Music' first published in *Illustrierte Rote Post*, March 1932, Berlin; reprinted in translation in *Hanns Eisler: A Rebel in Music* (Seven Seas Books, Berlin 1978, p. 59)
20 *ibid.*
21 Eisler, Hanns 'On Stupidity in Music' *ibid.*, p. 189
22 Willett, John *The Theatre of Bertolt Brecht* (Eyre Methuen, London 1967, 3rd edition, pp. 107-8)
23 Innes, C D *Erwin Piscator's Political Theatre* (Cambridge University Press, 1972, p. 30)
24 Piscator, Erwin 'New Red Stage' February 1932 quoted in Innes, *ibid.*, p. 31
25 Piscator, Erwin programme to *Hoppla, Wir Leben!* quoted in Innes, *ibid.*, p. 62
26 Innes, *ibid.*, p. 5
27 *ibid.*, p. 187
28 *ibid.*, p. 185
29 Vakhtangov quoted in Willett, *op.cit.*, pp. 111-2
30 Brecht, Bertolt letter to Piscator, March 1947 quoted in Innes, *op.cit.*, p. 198
31 *ibid.*, p. 198
32 *ibid.*, p. 25

CHAPTER 3

1 Heinsheimer, Hans *Menagerie in F Sharp* (T V Boardman & Co., New York 1949, p. 132)
2 Abravanel, Maurice *Le Protagoniste* reprinted in Drew, David (ed.) *Über Kurt Weill* (Suhrkamp Verlag, Frankfurt 1975, p. 18)
3 Heinsheimer, Hans *op.cit.*, p. 133
4 Heinsheimer, Hans *op.cit.*, p. 134, 136-7
5 Heinsheimer, Hans *op.cit.*, p. 137
6 Lenya, Lotte 'In Conversation with Steven Paul' in programme booklet for Kurt Weill (DGG 2740-153 p. 8)
7 quoted in Willett, John *Brecht on Theatre* (Eyre Methuen, London 1978, p. 86)
8 Weill, Kurt *Anmerkungen zu meiner Oper 'Mahagonny'* in Drew, David (ed.) *Kurt Weill: Ausgewählte Schriften* (Suhrkamp Verlag, Frankfurt 1975, p. 56)
9 Lenya, Lotte quoted in Friedrich, Otto *Before the Deluge* (Michael Joseph, London 1974, p. 262)
10 Drew, David 'The History of *Mahagonny*' (*Musical Times*, January 1963, p. 18)
11 Lenya, Lotte quoted in Friedrich, *op.cit.*, p. 262
12 Lenya, Lotte quoted in Padmore, Elaine 'Kurt Weill' (*Music & Musicians*, October 1972, pp. 35-6)
13 Friedrich, Otto *Before the Deluge*, *op.cit.*, p. 268
14 Aufricht, E J *Die Moritat vom Mackie Messer* (*Melos* 33, p. 359)

15 Lenya, Lotte quoted in Friedrich *op.cit.*, p. 265
16 see Aufricht, E J *op.cit.*, pp. 359-63
17 Heinsheimer, Hans *op.cit.*, p. 138
18 *ibid.*, p. 140
19 Lenya, Lotte quoted in Freidrich *op.cit.*, p. 270
20 Heinsheimer, Hans *op.cit.*, p. 140
21 Lenya, Lotte quoted in Friedrich *op.cit.*, p. 140
22 Heinsheimer, Hans *op.cit.*, p. 139
23 *ibid.*, p. 134
24 Lenya, Lotte quoted in Friedrich *op.cit.*, p. 271
25 quoted in Willett, John *op.cit.*, p. 85
26 Lenya, Lotte 'In Conversation with Steven Paul', *op.cit.*, p. 8
27 Heinsheimer, Hans *op.cit.*, pp. 146-7
28 Weill, Kurt *Notiz zum Berliner Requiem* in Drew, David (ed.) *Kurt Weill: Ausgewählte Schriften* (Suhrkamp Verlag, Frankfurt 1975, p. 139)
29 Brecht, Bertolt 'An Example of Pedagogics' in Willett, John *op.cit.*, p. 31
30 *ibid.*, p. 32
31 see Drew, David 'The History of *Mahagonny*', *op.cit.*, pp. 18-20
32 see Drew, David 'Notes to *Happy End*' accompanying *Happy End* recording (CBS 73463)
33 Lenya, Lotte quoted in Adam, Peter 'September Song' (*The Listener*, 24 May 1979, p. 707)
34 Lenya, Lotte 'In Conversation with Steven Paul', *op.cit.*, p. 19
35 see Drew, David 'Notes to *Happy End*', *op.cit*

CHAPTER 4

1 Weill, Kurt *Über meine Schuloper 'Der Jasager'* reprinted in Drew, David (ed.) *Kurt Weill: Ausgewählte Schriften* (Suhrkamp Verlag, Frankfurt 1975, pp. 61-3)
2 see Drew, David 'Weill's School Opera' (*Musical Times*, No 106, December 1964, p. 934)
3 Heinsheimer, Hans *Fanfare for Two Pigeons* (Doubleday & Co., New York 1954, p. 177)
4 see Drew, David *op.cit.*, p. 935
5 Warschauer, Frank 'Die Weltbühne' 8 July 1930, quoted in Ewen, Frederic *Bertolt Brecht* (Calder & Boyars, London 1967, p. 247)
6 Heinsheimer, Hans *Menagerie in F Sharp* (T V Boardman & Co., New York 1949, p. 174)
7 *ibid.*
8 *ibid.*, p. 173
9 *ibid.*, p. 175
10 Lenya, Lotte quoted in Friedrich, Otto *Before The Deluge* (Michael Joseph, London 1974, p. 328)
11 Lenya, Lotte 'September Song' (*The Listener*, 24 May 1979, p. 707)
12 Brecht, Bertolt reprinted in Willett, John *Brecht on Theatre* (Eyre Methuen, London 1978, p. 87)
13 Lenya, Lotte 'September Song' (*The Listener*, 24 May 1979, p. 708)
14 Völker, Klaus *Brecht: A Biography* (Calder & Boyars, London 1979, p. 59)
15 Willett, John *The Theatre of Bertolt Brecht* (Eyre Methuen, London 1967, 3rd edition, p. 156)

16 Brecht, Bertolt *Diaries 1920-1922* (Eyre Methuen, London 1979, p. 65)
17 *ibid.*
18 anonymous review, 9 March 1932, reprinted in Drew, David (ed.) *Über Kurt Weill* (Suhrkamp Taschenbuch, Frankfurt 1975, p. 77)
19 Zweig, Stefan *The World of Yesterday* (Cassell, London 1943, p. 361)
20 Bullock, Alan *Hitler: A Study in Tyranny* (Penguin Books, London 1962, p. 213)
21 *ibid.*
22 'L. St.' 20 February 1933 reprinted in Drew, David (ed.) *Über Kurt Weill*, *op.cit.*, p. 108
23 *Volkischer Beobachter* 24 February 1933, reprinted in *ibid.*, pp. 110-11
24 Milhaud, Darius *Notes without Music* (Alfred A Knopf, New York 1952, p. 236)
25 Vuillermoz, Émile *Candide* 15 December 1932, reprinted in Drew, David (ed.) *Über Kurt Weill*, *op.cit.*, p. 101
26 More, Marcel *La Politique* 1932 reprinted in *ibid.*, p. 98
27 Mehring, Walter 1933 reprinted in *ibid.*, p. 118)
28 Kessler, Count Harry *Tagebücher* reprinted in *ibid.*, p. 18
29 Huth, Anno *Der Weg der Verheissung* reprinted in *ibid.*, p. 122

CHAPTER 5

1 Lenya, Lotte 'September Song' (*The Listener* 24 May 1979, p. 708)
2 Atkinson, Brook *Broadway* (Cassell, London 1971, p. 342)
3 *ibid.*
4 *ibid.*
5 Weinraub, Bernard 'Lenya on Weill: The Memory Lingers On' (*New York Times*, 25 October 1964, 114:17 section 2)
6 see Drew, David 'Two Weill Scores' (*Musical Times*, September 1966, p. 798)
7 see Drew, David 'Kurt Weill and His Critics – 2' (*Times Literary Supplement* 10 October 1975, p. 1198)
8 Weill, Kurt 'Lunch Time Follies' reprinted in Drew, David (ed.) *Kurt Weill, Ausgewählte Schriften* (Surhkamp Verlag, Frankfurt 1975, p. 87)
9 see Willett, John *The Theatre of Erwin Piscator* (Eyre Methuen, London 1978, p. 153)
10 Carter, Elliot *The Writings of Elliot Carter* (Indiana University Press, Bloomington 1977, p. 95)
11 Drew, David 'Two Weill Scores', *op.cit.*, p. 789
12 Weill, Kurt 'A Musical Play About New York' reprinted in *Weill-Lenya* (Goethe House, New York 1976)
13 Lenya, Lotte quoted in Horowitz 'Lotte Lenya Recalls Weill's *Street Scene*' (*New York Times*, 26 October 1979)
14 *ibid.*
15 Downes Olin, quoted in Kowalke, Kim '*Street Scene*: A Broadway Opera' New York City Opera Playbill, 1979, p. 51
16 Weill, Kurt quoted in Drummond, Andrew H *American Opera Librettos* (Scarecrow Press Inc., Metuchen, New Jersey 1973, p. 107)
17 Heinsheimer, Hans *Menagerie in F Sharp* (T V Boardman & Co., New York 1949, p. 130)
18 Atkinson, Brook *New York Times* 6 November 1949, quoted in Drummond, Andrew H, *op.cit.*, p. 103
19 Barnes, Howard *New York Herald Tribune* 31 October 1949, quoted in Drummond, Andrew H, *ibid.*

20 Gibbs, Woolcott *New Yorker* 12 November 1949, quoted in Drummond, Andrew H, *ibid.*
21 Hewes, Henry *Saturday Review* 6 May 1972, p. 64

CHAPTER 6

1 Dallapiccola, Luigi, *Incontro con Anton Webern* Florence 1945, quoted in Moldenhauer, Hans *Anton Von Webern: A Chronicle of His Life and Work* (Gollancz, London 1978, p. 537)
2 *ibid.*
3 see Drew, David *First Symphony* notes accompanying Argo ZRG 755
4 Weill, Kurt 'Schoenberg: *Pierrot Lunaire*' reprinted in Drew, David (ed.) *Kurt Weill: Ausgewählte Schriften* (Suhrkamp Verlag, Frankfurt 1975, p. 124)
5 Weill, Kurt 'Arnold Schoenberg' reprinted in *ibid.*, pp. 119-20
6 Weill, Kurt 'Alban Berg: *Wozzeck*' reprinted in *ibid.*, p. 154
7 see Weill, Kurt 'Gustav Mahler: Symphony IX' reprinted in *ibid.*, pp. 121-2
8 see Drew, David 'After the First Symphony' notes accompanying Argo ZRG 755
9 Weill, Kurt, *Busoni und die neuen Musik* reprinted in Drew, David (ed.) *Kurt Weill: Ausgewählte Schriften*, *op.cit.*, pp. 20-1)
10 Dent, Edward *Ferruccio Busoni* (E Eulenberg, London 1974, p. 280 – reprint)
11 *ibid.*, p. 281
12 *ibid.*
13 Busoni, Ferruccio 'Young Classicism' *Frankfurter Zeitung*, 1920
14 see Kemp, Ian *Second Symphony* notes accompanying Argo ZRG 755

CHAPTER 7

1 see Drew, David 'Music Theatre in the Weimar Republic' *Proceedings of the Royal Musical Association* vol. 88 1962
2 'Interview with an Exile' reprinted in Willett, John *Brecht on Theatre* (Eyre Methuen, London 1978, p. 65)
3 *ibid.*, p. 86
4 Friedrich, Otto *Before the Deluge* (Michael Joseph, London 1974, p. 261)
5 *ibid.*
6 Brecht, Bertolt 'The Epic Theatre and Its Difficulties' in Willett, John *op.cit.*, p. 23
7 see Brecht, Bertolt 'The Modern Theatre is the Epic Theatre' in Willett, John, *ibid.*, pp. 33-42
8 see Dent, E. J. *Ferruccio Busoni* (E Eulenberg, London 1974, p. 305)
9 Busoni, Ferrucio 'Young Classicism' letter to *Melos* quoted in Slonimsky, N *Music Since 1900* (Cassell, London, 1971, fourth edition, p. 351)
10 Dent, E J *op.cit.*, p. 297
11 Weill, Kurt *Bekenntnis zur Oper* reprinted in Drew, David (ed.) *Kurt Weill: Ausgewählte Schriften* (Suhrkamp Verlag, Frankfurt 1975, p. 30)
12 Weill, Kurt *Busonis Faust und die Erneuerung der Operform*, reprinted in Drew, David, *ibid.*, pp. 31-2
13 *ibid.*, p. 31
14 *ibid.*, p. 32
15 Weill, Kurt *Aktuelles Theater*, reprinted in Drew, David, *ibid.*, pp. 48-9

16 this passage in *Der Protagonist* is discussed in detail in David Drew's 'Music Theatre in the Weimar Republic', *op.cit.*, pp. 98-9
17 Bie, Oskar *Der Protagonist* reprinted in Drew, David (ed.) *Über Kurt Weill* (Suhrkamp Taschenbuch, Frankfurt 1975, p. 15)
18 Abravanel, Maurice *Der Protagonist*, reprinted in Drew, David, *ibid.*, p. 18
19 Adorno, T W *Protagonist und Zar* reprinted in Drew, David, *ibid.*, p. 26
20 Stobel, Heinrich 'Kurt Weill 1920-27, reprinted in Drew, David, *ibid.*, p. 28
21 Weill, Kurt *Der Protagonist* reprinted in Drew,. David (ed.) *Kurt Weill: Ausgewählte Schriften, op,cit.*, p. 52
22 Drew, David 'The History of *Mahagonny*' *Musical Times*, January 1963, p. 18
23 Weill, Kurt *Aktuelles Theater* reprinted in Drew, David (ed.) *Kurt Weill: Ausgewählte Schriften, op.cit.*, p. 46
24 Weill, Kurt *Tanzmusik, Jazz* reprinted in Drew, David *ibid.*, pp. 132-3
25 Weill, Kurt *Notiz zum Jazz* reprinted in Drew, David, *ibid.*, pp. 132-3
26 Weill, Kurt *Notiz zum Berliner Requiem* reprinted in Drew, David, *ibid.*, pp. 139-40
27 Heinsheimer, Hans *Fanfare for Two Pigeons* (Doubleday & Co., New York 1954, p. 177)
28 Weill, Kurt *Aktuelles Zweigespräch über die Schuloper* reprinted in Drew, David (ed.) *Kurt Weill: Ausgewählte Schriften, op.cit.*, p. 67)
29 Adorno T W quoted in Drew, David 'The History of *Mahagonny*', *op.cit.*, pp. 21-2
30 Ewen, Frederic *Bertolt Brecht: His Life, His Art and His Times* (Calder & Boyars, London 1970, p. 113)
31 *ibid.*
32 Brecht, Bertolt quoted in Ewen, Frederick, *ibid.*, p. 66
33 from Feuchtwanger, 'Success' quoted in Ewen, Frederic, *ibid.*, p. 90
34 Adorno, T W *Zur Musik der Dreigroschenoper* reprinted in Drew, David (ed.) *Über Kurt Weill, op.cit.*, p. 42
35 Cocteau, Jean *Le Coq et L'Arlequin* translated by Myers, R (Egoist Press, Paris 1921)
36 Kemp, Ian 'Harmony in Weill: Some Observations' *Tempo* no. 104, 1973, p. 11
37 Kemp, Ian 'Second Symphony' notes accompanying recording of Weill's symphonies on Argo ZRG 755
38 Adorno, T W *Zur Musik der Dreigroschenoper* in Drew, David (ed.) *Über Kurt Weill, op.cit.*, pp. 39-44
39 Ewen, Frederic *op.cit.*, pp. 185-6
40 Drew, David 'Weill's School Opera' *Musical Times* no. 106, December 1964, p. 934
41 see Drew, David 'Topicality and the Universal: The Strange Case of Weill's *Die Bürgschaft, Music and Letters*, vol. 39, July 1958, pp. 242-55
42 see Drew, David, 'Weill's School Opera', *op.cit.*, p. 899
43 Weill, Kurt *Busonis Faust und die Erneuerung der Operform* reprinted in Drew, David (ed.) *Kurt Weill: Ausgewählte Schriften, op.cit.*, p. 35

CHAPTER 8

1 see Drew, David 'Two Weill Scores' *Musical Times*, September 1966, p. 798
2 Heyworth, Peter (ed.) *Conversations with Otto Klemperer* (Gollancz, London 1973, p. 64)
3 Weill, Kurt *Der Protagonist* reprinted in Drew, David (ed.) *Kurt Weill: Ausgewählte Schriften* (Suhrkamp Verlag, Frankfurt 1975, p. 53)

4 Weill, Kurt quoted in Kowalke's '*Street Scene*: A Broadway Opera' New York City Opera programme booklet, October 1979, p. 50
5 Hughes, Langston *My Collaboration with Kurt Weill* reprinted in German translation in Drew, David (ed.) *Über Kurt Weill* (Suhrkamp Taschenbuch, Frankfurt 1975, pp. 141-5)
6 Weill, Kurt 'A Musical Play About New York' reprinted in Marx, Henry (ed.) *Weill-Lenya* (Goethe House, New York, 1976)
7 Lenya, Lotte quoted in Horowitz, Joseph 'Lotte Lenya Recalls Weill's *'Street Scene'* *New York Times* 26 October 1979
8 Weill, Kurt 'The Future of Opera in America' quoted in Kowalke, *op.cit.*, p. 48
9 Thomson, Virgil *New York Tribune*, 9 April 1950
10 Chase, Gilbert 'America's music from the Pilgrims to the Present' quoted in Drummond *American Opera Librettos* (Scarecrow Press Inc., Metuchen, New Jersey 1973, p. 29)
11 Drew, David 'Two Weill Scores', *op.cit.*, p. 789
12 *ibid.*
13 see Lenya, Lotte 'September Song' *The Listener*, 24 May 1979, p. 708
14 see Horowitz, *op.cit.*
15 see Thomson, Virgil, *op.cit.*
16 Weill, Kurt letter to *Life Magazine* reprinted in Marx, Henry (ed.), *op.cit.*
17 Lenya, Lotte in Horovitz, *op.cit.*
18 Irwin Lew, Beth *George Grosz: Art and Politics in the Weimar Republic* (University of Wisconsin Press, Madison/London 1971, p. 233)
19 Lenya, Lotte 'September Song', *op.cit.*, p. 708

ACKNOWLEDGEMENTS

The publishers would like to thank the following for the loan of photographs and other illustrative material used in this book.

Akademie du Künste, Bertolt Brecht Archiv, Berlin-DDR.

BBC Hulton Picture Library.

Norman Bel Geddes Collection, Hoblitzelle Theatre Arts Library: Humanities Research Centre, University of Texas at Austin, by permission of the Executrix of the Norman Bel Geddes estate, Mrs Edith Lutyens Bel Geddes.

Bettman Archive Inc., New York.

Bildarchiv Preussischer Kulterbesitz, Berlin.

Casparius Collection, London.

Culver Pictures Inc., New York.

George Grosz Estate, Princeton, New Jersey.

Hoblitzelle Theatre Arts Library: Humanities Research Centre, University of Texas at Austin.

Robert Hunt Library, London.

Keystone, London.

Lichtbildwerkstatte Alpenland, Vienna.

Kugal Meyer – New York Public Library.

Photo Library Collection, Museum of City of New York.

Popperphoto, London.

The Post.

The Billy Rose Theatre Collection, New York Public Library.

Alison and Peter Smithson.

Springer/Bettman Film Archive, New York.

Maria Steinfeldt, Berlin-DDR.

Theatermuseum des Institute für Theaterwissenschaft der Universität Köln.

Theatre Collection, Museum of City of New York.

Ullstein, Berlin.

Universal Edition A. G., Vienna.

Roger Viollet, Paris.

Wilde World Photos, New York.

INDEX